EMANCIPATED LOVE JUNKIE

LIBERATING MYSELF FROM ANOREXIA

RACHEL WILSHUSEN

ACKNOWLEDGMENTS

For a family who loves me, exactly as I am.
And for Ry, whose support is behind the heart of this book.

PROLOGUE

I was a sweaty pig squeezed into spandex shorts and a washed-out sports bra. Wobbling on one leg, I pressed a hot right foot into a shaky left thigh. Without any friction, however, my foot slowly slid down my inner thigh and I clumsily toppled over on my mat.

Bright pink pig down!—I said to myself.

This is why women wear yoga pants. If I was wearing slimming Lulu pants, I wouldn't see my piggy thighs in this mirror.

"I invite you to spread your branches," a silky voice called from the back of the studio. Feeling more like a squatty shrub than a proud tree, I exerted myself once more to find the posture. Beads of sweat competed in races from my forehead into my eyes. Anxious to distract myself, I took stock of the studio's inventory. Apart from a tower of yoga blocks and hanging straps in a corner, only mats and bodies filled the space. That is except for one mega-buff, shirtless yogi sweating half his weight onto the floor. The lake on his mat was unsettling, but the studio's faux teakwood and exposed beams were comforting. Bare, clean, fresh, and empty: these were feelings I

1

craved in life and found in the polished aesthetics of studios and hipster cafes (which usually offered the additional benefit of banana bread).

The smooth talking instructor glided across the room to offer adjustments and refinement cues. I fixated on her graceful movements and lithe body. She was a Lululemon advertisement in a twisty pastel sports bra and dusky pink leggings. I wondered if she ever ate banana bread. "Switch and bring your left foot above your ankle or above your knee," she purred. "Shine your chest forward and come to your fullest expression. With every *inhale* consider what you want to bring into your life. With every *exhale*, release something that is holding you back."

I'm here for a completely new life! I'm here to look and feel exactly like you—clean and beautiful and perfect! Is that too much to ask?

Racing thoughts vied with physical exhaustion as we lay down and rolled our bodies into porcupine balls. Holding myself in as tightly as possible, I embraced all my familiar feels: anxiety, doubt, self-hate, and sadness. Tears mingled with sweat against my face and knees as the studio lights softly dimmed. Sweet Shavasana! I had survived ninety-minutes at 105 degrees F without consuming a morsel of food during the last ten hours. Settling into Corpse Pose, I succumbed to thoughts knocking on my consciousness.

I should be skinnier. I could be if I tried harder. I'm so hungry. I should have eaten something before class. But then I would feel like a beached whale now. Why am I on this mat again? Oh yeah, because I'm crazy and can't handle life.

At this moment of future tripping, the instructor pressed a fragrant eucalyptus towel against my forehead. The cold pressure on my burning temples felt heavenly. I was glad I'd forced myself to finish; the pain was worth this temporary peace. Back in the locker room, I quickly showered, pulled black tights over shaky legs, and forced a mass of hair into a crooked ponytail. Then, grabbing my bag, I ran into a strong wind that took my breath away. Toasty warm but starving at my core, I scurried down the street in search of something hot for dinner.

An hour later, my belly full of eats, I walked across the bridge to Courtney's apartment. I felt full—too full; disgusting in fact. I didn't deserve a heavy sandwich! I didn't deserve chips! And I surely didn't deserve a dreamy, pink cupcake! Tears welling up, I once again admitted I needed help.

~

Hi, I'm Rachel, and when it comes to food, it's complicated. For most of my life I have not been able to simply eat my food. It's not easy when a voice inside you is screaming—

Put down the cupcake, greedy piggy! What makes you think you deserve a cupcake?

The overwhelming challenge of eating and then sitting with a cupcake inside my belly led me to a hot yoga class in 2014. At least it was one of the reasons. On a wider level, I was sucking at keeping it together in Charleston, South Carolina. I was bawling my eyes out at the drop of a pin and sitting comatose in cars, too demotivated to button those hard to reach buttons. For twenty years I'd attempted to manage my anorexia and its corresponding anxiety with grace and dignity. Constantly moving, I took advantage of newness as a way to conceal my insecurities while engaging in destructive behavior. Our hearts, however, irrevocably linked to our minds and guts, can only take so much! After years of pushing my "true self" to the fringes, I broke. A final straw broke my brittle back and released wasp-y bottles of suppressed emotions that broke through the confines of my body and shattered onto the pavement like millions of tiny pieces of glass. Unable to squeeze my anger and deep-rooted, negative beliefs back into a tidy jar, I melted into a puddle of despair. Surveying the aftermath, I questioned if I could ever stand up again. But, as it always does —even after the bleakest of nights—the sun rose and offered hope to the hopeless. Picking myself off the floor, I straightened my hair, tied my Converse, and flew to Vancouver in search of a better life.

∾

This is the story of my eating disorder battle and subsequent journey towards Recovery. I'm not a spiritual guru—I still lace my gloves each morning to fight negative vibes—but having resurfaced from the anorexia gauntlet stronger than I ever thought possible, I hope my aha moments and truths will uplift your spirits and pin feelings of hope onto your heart! Moreover, sprinkling chapters with fresh insights and perspectives I've collected along my way, I entreat you to join me as an **_Emancipated Love Junkie—liberated from a destructive voice and passionately flooding your world with love._** As you disempower your inner critic to radiate your true self on a journey towards Recovery, you'll feel empowered to cultivate a love-centered existence that leads to health, happiness, and the emotional crème de la crème, JOY. Remember your glee when you were a tiny human, running half-naked through a sprinkler with a giant ice cream cone in one sticky fist? This book will help you to access that kind of goodness today, tomorrow, and for the rest of your life.

SECTION I: SWEET INNOCENCE

1

BEING A KID WAS MAGICALLY DELICIOUS

YUMA, ARIZONA: 1983

My early relationship with food was clovers, blue moons, and rainbows magically delicious. I arrived in Yuma, Arizona like a box of Nerds—split in half to facilitate a shot of strawberry followed by a shot of grape. Bright pink in the face from screaming, the doctor flipped me over to reveal a deep purple birthmark covering two-thirds of my bum. Hours later, my pink and purple person was swaddled and riding through the desert heat to start the great adventure of life.

I often wonder what might have happened if my dad hadn't left the Marines the following summer to start graduate school in Oregon. Would I have become a homegrown girl with roots in the southwestern soil? Would I have attended Arizona State and be posting pictures of my college sweetheart and our five kids on Instagram? Maybe I would have nurtured a simple reality and merrily soared through my twenties and thirties. Such alternate versions of our lives are conveniently filled with the best outcomes. When I look at my past rationally, however, I suspect I still would have fallen into thick cream along the way and struggled for years to churn my problems into deliciously sweet butter. Regardless, at six months I was whisked up north to commence a nomadic lifestyle in the homeland of Nike and Tillamook ice cream.

As a kid, I didn't realize my dad was a student, experimenting on cadavers by day and working at a funeral home by night to make ends meet. I'd naively inform school teachers he was unemployed and, when I dislocated my shoulder in the backyard, I hollered for my mom to take me to see a *real* doctor. This tantrum was surprisingly indulged, and, hours later, I was happily riding home with a readjusted shoulder and a cherry Popsicle. Being a mini American in the '80s was the bomb. The rules were simple: come home before dark, don't take candy from strangers (especially those sporting mustaches), and eat the food on your plate. I sustained low expectations regarding the plate I was meant to polish. Meals at our house met the Betty Crocker cheap and cheerful standard. Parmesan clumps in green cans spruced-up spaghetti, vegetables meant canned corn or green beans, and bread crumbs stuck to cheddar cheese uplifted the saddest of casseroles. While I disliked staring down a Campbell's split pea or black bean soup on occasion, I accepted wholesome dinners as my childhood cross to bear.

With my dad in school and three kids to feed, the impact of a sale on canned soups or any packaged foods was felt throughout the household. There was the winter we stocked our freezer with generic chocolate puddings that, once partially thawed, created a layer of skin on top I'd scrape off before plunging in my spoon. There was also the winter where we stored a crate of Captain Crunch's Christmas Crunch in closets and under beds due to a holiday special. In this case, I was awestruck by my two older brothers' creation of "swamp mug". Smashing crunch berries and milk together in the bottom of our bowls, we cheerfully ate our way through a red and green slog into the spring. And then there were the winters we'd sit down to a "Pop! Hiss!" medley at dinner as my mom opened a jar of peaches, bobbing around in their juices like animals trapped in formaldehyde.

Raised in a Latter Day Saint (Mormon) household, my mom gleefully took on board the fruit preservation aspect of our pioneer heritage. Like a Miss Chiquita, but without the Latina flair, she'd boil sugar and spices, simmer berries into syrupy substances, and roll out miles of fruit leather. Although her dried and canned selections were impressive, the aromas of pies, crumb bars, and other fruity bombshells browning in the oven filled my heart with delight. During summer holidays, I became an industrious Strawberry Shortcake, plucking thousands of berries in the wild before dusting their bodies with sugar in our Berry Bitty Cafe. Adhering to the "one for me, one for the pail" policy as I laced my way through strawberry fields, I'd proudly return home scratched, stained, and burnt like Strawberry Crisp.

By August, I was poised for the ultimate challenge in U-Picking: blackberries. I don't mean the pathetic, six-ounce cartons sold in stores for $5.95! I mean massive amethyst beauties, bursting with flavor after reaching their juice capacity in the hot sun. While local bushes on our poor side of town were plentiful, my main employment occurred at my grandparents' house, five hours north across the Canadian border.

Sticking rakes, gloves, and a rickety ladder out the back of my grandparents' car, we'd drive past the outskirts of town and into an enchanted forest of bushes overloaded with gems. Readjusting my baseball cap, I'd race out of the car with my pail swinging on my arm, determined to let no berry in sight shrivel and die. My mom tackled the most dangerous work, leaning our ladder against a sturdy bush and stepping up with a rake in hand to reach the loftiest branches. I understood her willingness to risk her life for the best of the season as I stripped low hanging boughs of heavy clusters, immune to sharp thorns that drew blood beneath the surface of my clothes. Once our pails were filled beyond capacity, we'd return home for my grandpa and I to sift through hordes of scrubbed up beauties in preparation of their final act. My grandpa always opted for a giant bowl of vanilla ice cream overloaded with berries. I preferred to wait as my gram blended cream and berries together into a lavender milkshake. Freshly showered and sucking ice-cold berry bits on their porch, life was unabashedly perfect.

~

Winter arrives early in Oregon. Every October 31st, I'd race out the door with my witch costume barely fitting over my parka to scour the neighborhood for SweeTARTS, Laffy Taffys and bite-size Butterfingers. Channeling the Cheshire Cat, I'd exhale circles of breath high into the darkness while keeping an eye out for early snowflakes. Inevitably, thick flakes appeared ahead of Turkey Trots and I'd rush the season by decking our halls with red garlands and festive window stickers. My mom's canning skills are impressive, but it's baking where the women in our family triumph, and Christmas was the coup de gras. What our holiday parties lacked in spiked punch my mother compensated for with towers of cookies and bars highlighting the season's finest fillings, frostings, whipped creams, crusts, and glazes. I gazed in admiration as my mom transformed into a Christmas angel on these nights, shining in glittery dresses and high heels as she rushed to fill this glass and replace that tray of treats. As Andy Williams clicked off on our cassette player and my dad hunted down rogue scarves and coats, I'd watch from the window as my mom embraced departing guests who rushed into the cold moonlight with a rosy, sugary glow. She was the hostess of my dreams and I planned to someday smell, look, and act exactly like her.

Most years, we'd devour scads of my mom's bakes before driving up the coast to gobble-up my gram's holiday desserts. With bars and cookies dancing in our heads, we'd cram into Rosie, our loyal station wagon, and I'd sing "Over the River and Through the Woods" on repeat, until an older brother ordered me to cut it out. It wasn't a sleigh, but I felt the enchantment of a winter wonderland as whirling snowflakes landed on my window. Once we arrived, I'd rush up the steps in pursuit of grandparent kisses and my gram's Royal Dansk tin that only appeared at Christmas. This was the tin filled with two layers of butter cookies, snugly layered in white, ruffled sleeves. I didn't realize every cookie—regardless of shape— was made of the exact same dough; consequently, I felt certain the pretzel variety were the tastiest.

Although I flaunted an unbridled love of desserts, I wasn't blind to bodies and weight. On the contrary, I was frightened by fatness and shied away from chubby family friends who seemed intent on acquiring hugs from small girls. For the time being, however, even without a pair of LA Gear kicks to up my four square swagger, I was a happy and uninhibited superstar. With a sporty side matching a solid set of brains, I quickly realized there are gold stars (rewards and prizes) for being the best, and that I could reach my ponytail high above this bar. Staring at sparkly stars one chilly summer night as my eldest brother Shawn pointed out the Big and Little Dippers, my heart was struck by their glorious perfection. I subconsciously resolved to shine bright like a diamond in every facet of life as a perfect daughter, a perfect sister, a perfect student, a perfect pianist, and, someday, a perfect hostess in glitzy dresses and high heels.

SELF-LOVE GEM: SEE WITH CHILDHOOD EYES

As small children we see the world as a wondrous and beautiful place. As we grow older and encounter judgements and stings, however, many of us develop an inner voice that leaks fear into our minds and pushes our essence—our true self—to the fridges. We become stuck in a war with our critic for years, attempting to manifest strength while often feeling like a fraud who is undeserving of Kudos or happiness. Thankfully, with understanding and support (as outlined in the following chapters) we can release our inner critic to once more see the world through our joyful, childhood eyes.

2

PASTEL EXPOSURE
AUGUSTA, GEORGIA: AGE 9

Packing up Melissa Bunny, Care Bear, and a pink Corvette of Barbies to move across the country was confusing yet thrilling. Although I wasn't sure why we were moving to Georgia, I loved the fuss family friends were making over our departure. Sadly, our station wagon Rosie was not able to make such a taxing drive. After bawling my eyes out when my brother clarified this meant she was heading to the junkyard for dismemberment, I regrouped to welcome a shiny silver minivan into our family. Eager to showcase our upcoming adventure, my dad spread a Rand McNally map across the dining room table and drew sweeping lines across thousands of miles. Assessing the breadth of America, I believed drawing a straight line from Oregon to Georgia far more prudent, but I accepted "Dad knows best" and headed into the kitchen where I felt my skills were best appreciated.

My initial hopes of a McDonald's themed trip evaporated as I discovered an assembly line of peanut butter, strawberry freezer jam, and Wonder Bread slices waiting to be stuck together while my mom sectioned-off grapes and potato chips into baggies. Although denied a Happy Meal lineup, a few soft-serve cones along the way kept my spirits up for hours—or at least until the next pit-stop. As we crossed into Georgia and a flat canvas of pastels replaced colorful mountains, I rolled down my window to inhale a heavy, southern breeze. The heat felt marvelous against my cheek, especially considering I'd been promised a pool excursion as soon as we arrived at our hotel on base. I wasn't sure what to expect from Georgia, but as I dove into a cold pool hours later, channeling Ariel as I whipped my hair about under the water, I knew this was the start of a very big adventure.

~

Fort Gordon's muted tones mimicked the skins of peaches: light creams, sandy oranges, creamy pinks, and tawny browns. Like other Captain rank families, we moved into a small yellow duplex to share walls with two golden retrievers whose soft coats coordinated with the landscape. Our first chance to ditch our parents and a mountain of moving boxes, my brother Brandon and I set out on our bikes to explore the base's scene. The faint whir of spoke baubles sounded in my ears as I spotted camouflaged soldiers blending into nondescript buildings; how odd, I mused, that everyone wanted to dress like my dad. I peddled quickly to keep up, following Brandon as he jumped a curb onto the Baskin Robbins parking lot. As my brother weaved a lock through our bikes, I questioned his spontaneous decision. Surely our mom would know we'd ruined our appetites! But then, as we walked into a gust of AC and smelled sugar cones baking, I determined a new appetite *must* appear before dinner. After agonizing over options, I copy-catted Brandon's choice and tucked into a large scoop with a pretty pink spoon. As I smoothed the sides of my ice cream and encountered almond, chocolate, and marshmallow bits, I concluded Rocky Road is superior to all other flavors and that Georgia must be a splendid place to live.

Ventures beyond base brightened my pastel impressions of the south. Although Low Country Boils, with crawfish dumped across tablecloths, and Civil War excursions were unnerving events, I loved sighting dusty trucks flying unfamiliar flags and giant hounds out the back. I was also mesmerized by tanned women with acrylic nails and syrupy drawls sorting through okra and collard greens at our local grocery store. In Georgia, I concluded, women could ooze whatever aura they liked: Fila kicks and Braves jersey sporty, bronzed and skintight dress sultry, or even Daisy Dukes and crop top bare. I became aware of my own identity the day I pulled my fourth grade class photo out of a large white envelope. Dead center—amongst a sea of jean shorts, Keds, and black hair—I grinned as a vision of whiteness in a Sunday School dress and white lace socks and sandals. I can only assume this picture delighted my classmates' parents. Personally, I was mortified. Pulling on a swimsuit and grabbing my mom's *Good Housekeeping*, I headed to our deck in hopes of turning my skin a lovely caramel hue.

Seriously lacking in modern resources, qualified teachers, and cool playground equipment, Terrace Manor Elementary reeked of destitution. Standing like an ant hill upon a bed of red clay, even the foundations were rotten. White lace socks didn't stand a chance against clouds of dust that flew in through the windows to shroud window sills and classroom tiles in a chalky film. Mrs. Bing was a large, stylish woman who coordinated the burgundy hues of her nail polish with the dust on her heels, and rolled peppermints around in her mouth throughout the day. While I was amused by the red and white stripes that flickered through her teeth, I was fascinated by her approach to eating fried chicken. Gingerly picking a seasoned drumstick out of a container, she'd pull her lips forward to sink her teeth into the meat, pause for a moment, and then disengage, moving her whole body back to sit upright. Mrs. Bing earned a reputation as a softie due to her progressive views on corporal punishment. She was however, a champion of a school-wide initiative requiring students to carry cards to be marked in red if we spoke out of turn. As a terrified perfectionist, my card was free of shameful marks, which meant I was allowed to play trashcan basketball for tootsie rolls on Fridays. The plastic chew was satisfying, but I missed bartering homemade cookies for Bugles, a Twinkie, or a Swiss Roll at lunch. Trading at Terrance Manor was an underground market and sugar talk was limited to the school snack shop. Although I was the poster child of model behavior, it never occurred to me to ask my parents for change. Consequently, I watched with bitter envy as kids bit into giant dill pickles and stripped Airhead wrappers to create soft indentations in smooth taffy.

I was gutted to miss out on Airheads, but thrilled to skipout of selling Symphony Chocolate Bars over the summer to raise dollars for a school trip. My dad was officially employed as a *real* military doctor and we were moving to a base in Germany. That is until a cheeky brown recluse spider created an indentation in my butt for *his* snack. I was rushed to the hospital and commanded to drop my shorts in front of a supercute doc who verified the horror: my lavender birthmark was now a magenta welt overtaking both cheeks. I was mortified; my first show of skin in front of a man was this?

Fortunately, this humiliation was offset by pool excursions as my parents waited for my buttocks to chill out. The temperature drop from the high-dive into the water below felt incredible; spinning and leaping into the air I felt like Olympian Dorothy Poynton—but in a prettier aqua suit. As my brothers and I wasted entire days horsing around in the water, Cool

Ranch Doritos replenished our salts and tubes of coconut creams kept us safe from Georgia's mighty rays. When at last the final whistle blew, we'd load wet bodies and towels into our minivan, beat and ready to devour something scrumptious. On lucky evenings, dinner meant piles of deep-fried Elephant Ears. Assuming fork duty near the stove, I'd stand at attention with goggle impressions around my eyes and a mop of wet hair dripping on the floor, attentively waiting as my mom dropped large pale ovals into our electric skillet. The shocked dough created a glorious sizzle as it stretched and expanded until translucent bubbles rose in the middle and it was time. *Flip it now!* Expertly turning ear after ear in boiling oil, I'd watch with pride as a stack of warm, sugary beauties appeared on the counter. Too hot to stay indoors, I'd follow my bros onto our patio to overload my plate with crispy craters filled with strawberry freezer jam. And then, clean, safe, and cool, I'd close my eyes and bite into heaven as chatter about our upcoming adventure competed with the neighborhood crickets.

3

FROM ELEPHANT EARS TO BERLINERS

BAUMHOLDER, GERMANY: AGE 10

Once my bum returned to its lavender hue, I travelled across the Atlantic to hit jetlag at a million miles an hour. Without Ikea to educate us yet, I'd never heard of a duvet and found sleeping under clouds of cotton as divine as the smells of breaded pork and fries wafting under our door from the hotel kitchen below. After falling in and out of dream-states for countless hours, I was gently nudged by my mom. "Pull on a t-shirt and shorts, Rach. Let's find some breakfast." A fresh aroma of coffee and lemon cleaner lifted my stupor as we headed down the stairs and out the door, following cobblestone streets until we arrived at a bakery decorated with little red flowers out front. Busier than a Starbucks morning rush inside, scores of women were pointing to this and that while plucking change out of their purses. Looking every which way, I spotted bread and pastries emerging from massive ovens as golden, domed masterpieces. Outshining rows of white loaves perched high on shelves, batches of donuts—dusted with sugar or leaking out custards— waited to be selected from behind a glass counter. Now very much awake with a growling belly to feed, I eagerly pointed to the jewel in the bakery's crown: jelly-filled Berliners. My mom stretched her hand out firmly for a stout worker to pick out the right coins as a bag was filled with donuts and twisted on both ends. Picking out the top two as we headed towards our hotel, we bit into soft dough, bursting with jammy sweetness.

Berliners are every bit as nice as American Elephant Ears; I will be happy here.

~

My extroverted personality took flight in Germany as I collected friends and gold stars at school while occasionally indulging my sweet tooth with Berliners. Noticing jelly donut pudge on my friends as we sunbathed one day, however, I opened an exercise studio in our basement to cast out the fat from amongst us. As Tamilee Webb's *Buns of Steel* video commanded "Tiny pulses ladies!" to Madonna's "Holiday", I yelled "feel the burn!" to the weaker members of class. Unaware of the calories in/calories out concept, classes ended with a stop at the kitchen to replenish our fuel with cookies, which resulted in fairly limited weight loss results.

With time to spare between school and studio sessions, I emulated my mom by testing out my baking prowess. There were some definite fails, but a clean release of a Poppy Seed Cake from a Bundt and palatable Blondie Brownies resulted in a decision to enlist in the Girl Scouts. Their ethos was commendable, but once I realized I was meant to sell cookies, rather than bake them, I cancelled my membership. This seemed like a particularly smart decision since I was enrolling in a combined junior high/high school and feared resembling a Thin Mint in my Juniors uniform might stunt my popularity. I never reached the coolness I was after, but racing through

German villages with my upperclass brother Brandon in our Ford Probe while listening to (*What's the Story*) *Morning Glory?* felt awesome. Confident and extroverted, I knew my imminent arrival at school guaranteed banter with girlfriends, followed by a peppering of praise throughout the day. As a rising superstar, I was soon killing it academically and hustling my way up trumpet seats in the high school band.

Riding on a barrel wave of success, I believed perfection was a realistic life goal. Cross-country races throughout the autumn further verified that with hard work and perseverance, I could soar into the heavens to dwell amongst the stars. I loved every moment my sneakers sailed along German paths, lined with colorful ash trees and clusters of cows. As cool breezes moved through my ponytail, I'd inhale the earthy scent of leaves and mud, and experience a strong sense of peace and freedom. Alongside communing with nature, a crush on a German teammate with silky Vidal Sassoon hair and muscular arms and legs stoked my passion for running. Sending my budding hormones into the stratosphere, my heart beat with unrequited thrills as he sprinted into the finish to win his 5K races. My heart also pounded vigorously as I anticipated the start of my own race. The starting gun provided an invigorating jolt, and, although I was a pathetic sprinter relegated to the back, I'd pick girls off one by one like a bird of prey. Each time my ponytail swished past a weaker member of the flock, I'd lengthen my stride and pump my arms until I gloriously sped through the finish. Exploding with feelings of exhaustion and accomplishment, I'd commit to running all the faster and harder the following week. Any starting line jitters were an essential price to pay in pursuit of the finish line feeling.

Germany hits its peak in wintertime when charming red-roofed towns transform into snow globe wonderlands. Large snowfalls meant amassing mountains of snowballs to send flying into the air before tromping home with friends for cocoa while our mittens and scarves dried on heaters. Snow also meant the start of the Christkindl markets, when town centers transformed into pop-ups for Santa's workshop. Wandering through brightly lit stalls showcasing Christmas wreaths and intricate ornaments on cold December nights, I'd search for presents while the rich aromas of sausages, mulled wine, and roasting nuts ignited my appetite. After feasting on a white sausage twice the length of the roll attempting to cradle its body, I'd fill any remaining dessert spots in my belly with Lebkuchen, soft gingerbread cookies with a smooth base and domed top. Then, breathing heat into cold mittens, I'd watch through falling snow as a brass band lofted "Silent Night" and "O Christmas Tree" into the air.

Once the Christkindl pop-up markets transformed back into humble fruit and vegetable stands, and the last Lebkuchen disappeared from its tin, our movers arrived to send us packing. As we had years before, Brandon and I escaped an afternoon of cardboard boxes and moving mayhem to zoom off in our Ford Probe. Cracking open a packaged box of Oatmeal Cream Pies, we cruised through Little Debbie's finest bakes while reminiscing about our lives to the Cranberries' *No Need to Argue* CD. "Oh my life is changing every day, in every possible way..." O'Riordan cried out—and she was right. Time was moving fast and soon I would suppress my joyful self to welcome an inner critic into my mind. I've often wished I could return to these simple Oatmeal Cream Pie and Lebkuchen days, before I was struck by a snowstorm of anxiety and its snowdrifts of self-hate and despair. I was an overachieving perfectionist with high standards and ambition, but I was comfortable in my skin, confident in my relationships, and happy in my heart.

4

HOW A TIGHT SKIRT ROCKED MY WORLD

BOSTON, MASSACHUSETTS: AGE 14

M y dad's one-year Public Health program at Harvard on the Army's dime meant moving from a two-story German house into a small, urban apartment. My teenage senses ran riot amongst a sudden blitz of American pop culture and fast food, but after years of living on a sequestered base I was all sorts of jumpy about starting high school in Boston. Consequently, when my parents suggested I try out for preseason soccer to make friends before the first school bell sounded, I leapt at the opportunity.

∾

I stood on unfamiliar turf wearing an oversized jersey and a boxy pair of shorts. A flock of ponytails were already in the middle of a header drill when a sporty man with a whistle jostling around his neck strided over to say hello. I knew preseason was a few weeks underway, but I couldn't understand why I was late for practice today.

Great start, Rach.—I sarcastically noted.

Peering at the girls as the coach extended a firm hand, I gasped—this couldn't possibly be the right field; this was clearly a college cheerleading squad practice! My nerves skyrocketed as I assessed a field brimming with tanned shoulders and legs, fitted tanks and shorts, perfectly set mascara and blush, and mature yet slim, beautiful bods. Upon closer inspection, I would have noticed a fair amount of pimples, unkempt eyebrows, and badly cut bangs. En masse, however, I was walking onto the set of *Mean Girls* and I was Janis Ian, but far less cool. Coach Ken was the team's cherry on top. Tall, dark, and unequivocally hot, Ken was somewhere around thirty years old with thick black locks he ran his hand through while explaining drills. I have no clue why he took the job, but he was intent on coaching a winning team and on flirting with the cutest, underage girls on the field—particularly Sylvia. I couldn't blame him; she deserved to be worshipped! Her dark Mediterranean features perfectly offset a smooth complexion and flushed pink cheeks. Straight chestnut highlights added dimension to her look and I stared with admiration as she twirled her mane into an easy bun with a thin elastic band while Coach Ken shouted out directions. "Alright ladies, drop everything and head out the back. Let's see how you all do with this week's race. I'm expecting quick paces today; no half-baked efforts!"

I followed the girls off the field and across the road as I absorbed this new travesty. A race right now? Was this guy serious? After two months of shuffling around moving boxes while sucking down berry milkshakes and crunching on Blast O Butter popcorn during *Titanic* matinees, a two-mile race could not sound less appealing. As we shot-off down a path to circumnavigate a lake, I attempted to channel my cross-country spirit, focusing on one buttery blonde tail ahead as I huffed and puffed my way around the lake. Gasping for breath and sweating like a beast, however, my attempts were futile—I crossed dead last. Last!? How could this happen? I'd never come anywhere near last before! Choked up with failure as we walked back to the field, I anxiously looked for a way to salvage my pride.

Do something! Talk to someone; anyone! Don't let anyone see you're a scared rabbit.

I sidled up to the buttery blonde ponytail and attempted small talk. Although she responded with friendly chatter, I couldn't relate to her pop references or her commentary on "men". Apart from crushing on upperclassmen, I'd barely considered guys, much less played dirty with any in the back of beat-up cars or movie theaters. Back in America, it seemed, girls my age were mature, worldly, and, consequently, entirely out of my league. Over the ensuing weeks, my initial intimidation of the soccer Barbies and their Ken leader spiraled into full-blown terror. Shaking in my blue jersey and boots from northwestern breezes and teenage anxiety, I dutifully warmed the bench for the rest of the season.

My first month at school was equally disastrous. Amongst a sea of tall brown boots and fitted peacoats, I arrived for the first day wrapped in a giant Adidas parka and sporting neon green sneakers. Sixty seconds on the school grounds confirmed wearing sportswear five times your size is totally not cool; my entire wardrobe required instant burning. Attempting to hide in plain sight, I awkwardly shuffled about as I waited for the doors to open. As freshmen girls reunited with shrieks and hugs and described their Nantucket holidays and saucy summer flings, I painstakingly watched the minutes creep by on my watch. 7:56, 7:57, still 7:57...

Freak, are those girls looking at me? They're looking at my ridiculous coat, right? Do I look that stupid? Can we move apartments and switch school districts tomorrow?

Just when I felt I might keel over from stress, the bell sounded and I walked inside to face the day. Unfortunately, although I gradually assimilated into my classes and smiled at my Barbie crew in the hallways, my anxiety levels peaked from bell to bell as the afternoon and then subsequent days rolled by. Spooked but determined to play it cool, bathrooms presented a sanctuary from social suicide—a hiding place to escape the judgmental lunchroom milieu and painstaking ten-minute breaks between classes while also avoiding the mark of "total loser". Breathing in deeply to calm manic insides as I stared at my smudgy reflection in sink mirrors and washed my clean hands once more, I reminded myself the day would eventually be over. Soon I would be free of the flips in my belly and unbearable social awkwardness! In a matter of hours I'd be walking home with Alanis, Meredith, Sheryl, and Jewel spinning on my Discman for company! And yet, '90s pop icons and cold Boston air could not overcome a growing angst in my heart as golden leaves spiraled in clusters towards the pavement and Coach Ken advised I try a different sport the following year.

My mom sensed something was up and suggested over spaghetti one night we drop into J. Crew to see about some new clothes. This was massive. Mall excursions often involved us splitting a cinnamon and sugar explosion from Cinnabon. But a trip with a Visa ready to swipe? This was a rare and glorious event, which I honored by daydreaming of cute boots, tops, and scarves until the blessed day arrived and I drifted into J.Crew's cashmere-cotton heaven bursting with excitement. Admiring perfectly proportioned mannequins dressed in crisp white shirts, wooly fall sweaters, and structured blazers, my eyes darted up, down, and all around. I wanted *everything*. Quickly working my way around the store, I picked up this top and those pants, this skirt and that matching blouse. Then, hidden under an armful of clothes, I stumbled towards the dressing room with my mom in tow.

I popped a polka-dot top over my head and looked into the mirror. Cute, but no. I tried one after another, but every top was too flowy, tight, blah, or wide in the arms. "None of them do that much for you," my mom confirmed. I let out a heavy sigh and reached towards an assortment of skirts. The first was a navy number with buttons down the front and a hidden side-zip. I anxiously held onto both sides and pulled the fabric over my calves, thighs—and stopped. I yanked this way and that and sucked in the entirety of my gut, but it was useless; my body refused to squeeze through the hole! I looked at the tag, horrified—this was the larger of the two sizes I'd pulled from the rack. Hot tears rolled down my face as I vulnerably opened the door. My mom's answer? The clothes were to blame. Not to worry: she would rustle up some cute skirts on our ancient sewing machine in a jiffy! "Besides," she asserted, "J. Crew clothes aren't made nearly as well as they should be for their price; the company should be ashamed!"

My head reeled from this additional calamity. It was true, then; I was destined to be a loner without girlfriends (or a boyfriend, obviously) who wears homemade skirts, sucks at sports, and is excluded from parties.

I am a loser.

Tossing a heap of cotton rejects on the return rack, I walked outside the glass doors as a changed girl. Sure, I was already teetering on a self-confidence ledge, but now, after years of believing I was a rising star in the heavens, I sailed across the sky, precipitously losing self-worth until I landed as a pile of stardust. Whereas my youthful jitters and wobbles arose from a desire to advertise my awesomeness, from this moment onwards fear propelled my anxiety forward. My mind filled with doubt, disillusionment, and self-hate, I began to view physical perfection as the only way to prove my worth.

~

I sustained a fierce desire for Beauty throughout the rest of high school. For the next two years in succession, my dad's role as medical doc moved us to bases in Washington State and then Oklahoma. Watching a school disappear in the distance was nearly as exhilarating as the horror of another first day of school. First days always kicked off with strangers peering in my direction as I checked-out a new batch of cheerleaders, jocks, nerds, goths, and enviable "Sylvias". Sweet and charismatic, with a cool edge, friendly vibe, and effortless yet trendy fashion ensembles, Sylvias succeeded in all facets of life to receive praise, love, and attention from adults and the entire student body alike. Always the new girl, I stood out in a far less desirable way: as an easy target for unfiltered, hormonal banter. Anxious to survive lame scrubs—like a sophomore who called out "look at that girl's butt!" across the atrium—I oozed false confidence at pep-rallies, Homecoming dances, and, most importantly of all, the cafeteria. Beelining towards a table of soccer girls the first time I entered the boxed milk and tater-tot fray became a surefire way to save my bacon for the rest of the year, without resorting to hiding in bathrooms or quick laps around the campus.

Except when I was ditched. It didn't happen constantly; usually I was safe with my tablemates. An occasional ditch, however, cut through my heart like a knife and shook my sense of security. Would my friends be there tomorrow? Would I be forgotten again and miss out on a Chick-fil-A run? I naturally absorbed their mindlessness as my fault. If I was cute, with just a spark of Sylvian coolness, I would be slurping a frozen lemonade in the back of a friend's truck rather than racing out of the cafeteria doors in a panic. In reality, most of us are out for Numero Uno, and teenagers, riddled with insecurities and focused on their own reputations, are the very worst. Consequently, although I was well-liked and reclaiming my sportiness on the soccer field, it was easy as pie for new friends to forget the nice but quiet blonde.

After months of missed frozen lemonades, I rejoiced when the end arrived. Desperate to halt daily heart attacks, I'd repeatedly petitioned guidance counselors to skip a grade. My request was finally accepted and consequently, in 2000 I graduated as a free bird, gleefully flying out of my high school cage forever. It hadn't been all bad; I'd spent three years flipping through happy memories in Target parking lots after processing black and yellow rolls of film. With fear in charge, however, happiness had come in fleeting bursts rather than as a constant stream of goodness, which resulted in a silent wishing away of my teenage years.

As I metaphorically dropped a mic in my high school cafeteria and walked out, I looked towards the future with a hopeful heart, intent on proving my worth as a bright star in the night sky. Academically, this meant applying to Ivy League schools to keep-up with my older brother heroes attending Columbia and Cornell in New York. Socially, this meant rising above my anxieties to become a groovy chick, which underneath a layer of insecurities I still believed myself to be.

SELF-LOVE GEM: ACCEPT BEAUTIFUL IMPERFECTION

It's tempting to put complete strangers—celebrities, self-help gurus, women in our yoga class—on pedestals. It's easy to think someone is perfect and "has it all" when we know nothing about their world.

Interestingly, it's when we recognize others as the imperfect people they are that our love for them increases. Imperfect people are relatable; we are able to connect to their experiences and move beyond a shallow impression to forge deep and lasting relationships. And yes, it goes both ways! As you exude your authentic self, others will be drawn to your beautifully flawed spirit.

SECTION II: BINGING FOR BEAUTY

5

HOW CAKE BECAME MORE THAN CAKE

ELIZABETHTOWN, PENNSYLVANIA: AGE 17

Autumn runs through rural Pennsylvania filled my nose with more fragrances than a Yankee seasonal candle line. Breathing heavily in my Elizabethtown cross-country sweatshirt and tight ponytail, the aroma of damp leaves underfoot evoked yanking gooey guts out of pumpkins, sprinting down soccer fields, and popping pecan pies into the oven. Depending on the direction of a strong wind, I'd catch whiffs of manure or chocolate melting at the nearby Hershey factory. This interplay of related yet distinct smells was disconcerting. Examining country cows along my path, I'd either shoot the herd a disgusted "how could you!" look or crave a silvery, chocolate Kiss. If Kiss cravings circled through my mind, I'd soon be dreaming of hot cocoa and apple cider donuts, just like the ones I saw advertised on Amish stands along my route. By the time I rounded a final curve towards college, I'd inevitably be jonesing for hot eats and a mouthful of festive treats.

～

I left home as a zealous seventeen-year-old, ready to feel the Ivy League heat thousands of miles away from Oklahoma and friends who ditch. After rejections from Princeton and Yale, however, I postponed my aspirations to attend a small school in Pennsylvania. Elizabethtown College was a game changer. Within a week, I secured a freshman clique that ate every meal together and spent the minutes between lectures shacked-up in the coziest room in the hall. As we'd rattle on about upper-classmen hotties, I'd sit cross legged on the floor, twisting Keebler sandwiches to lick off the fudge before sticking the vanilla cookies back together. Although I was sweatpants level comfortable, however, I began to notice a smidge of pudge here and an extra bit of jelly roll there. I wasn't drinking cheap Coors Lights and I wasn't licking *that* much fudge off cookie sandwiches. Consequently, I turned my attention to the obvious culprit: the college cafeteria. An endless smorgasbord of eats was electrifying for a girl with a list of ED (eating disorder) symptoms:

- An overachieving perfectionist with OCD tendencies
   - A history of social isolationism and geographical displacement
   - Intense religious and academic standards
   - A negative perspective on appearance

Without question, "disordered eating" was my main point of entry into first bulimia, and then anorexia. Disordered eating is a common behavioral issue; as omnipresent as avocado slices on a hipster street taco menu. It's endless fads and dieting. It's taking down Ben & Jerrys with a serving spoon after a break-up. It's mindlessly scarfing a bag of Doritos while streaming

Warner Bros' *Stranger Things*. It's telling your coworkers about your amazing health regimen while sneaking mini Snickers bars under your desk, and praying no one sniffs-out the peanuts. Disordered eating stems from a myriad of sources. Maybe it was a parent obsessed with diets when you were growing up. Maybe food has been your emotional crutch for as long as you can remember. Or perhaps you simply struggle with willpower.

In my case, a disappearance of fixed rituals laid a bread-crumb trail to a mixed-up and backwards relationship with food. After a lifetime of Malt-O-Meal or Corn Flakes (frosted when lucky) at 5:45 a.m. and portioned out dinners served at 6:00 p.m., I abruptly became an autonomous food agent. My parents assumed I was emotionally and educationally equipped to feed myself properly when I headed out the door. This was not the case! Although I recognized Twinkies shouldn't head-line at meals, my nutritional understanding was based on the 1980s USDA food pyramid. Remember this iconic graphic? A whole loaf of french bread on the bottom, a glass of milk, a roasted chicken, and gold and white dots representing fats and sugars near the top? Apart from a rudimentary "broccoli= good, ice-cream= bad" and a rooted belief in the superiority of carbs, I was clueless on how to fuel my body. Consequently, when presented with a ticket for endless rigatoni and tater-tots, cakes and bread puddings soaked in mysterious creams, I belly flopped hard into a pool of neon blue Fruitopia and a lifestyle of disordered eating. An abhorrence of gluttony kept me in check, but empty carbs inevitably stole the dinner show. Snatching a Chocolate-Chip Bagel on the way out the door, I'd carry it upstairs like a clutch for a tasty late-night snack, assuming its ingredients and nutritional facts closely matched my mom's recipe for homemade Chocolate-Chip Cookies.

Rather than hiding under a patchwork quilt of fitness magazines, the latest diets, and hearsay, a foray into modern and accredited nutritional research will allow you to take charge of your health. As you learn how your belly processes and distributes energy throughout your body, you'll feel empowered to make informed nutritional choices and to limit the influence of an ignorant inner voice that might not have your interests at heart. Rather than viewing calories as dangerous numbers, focus on the nutrients to be gleaned from an apple, a square of lasagna, or a slice of banana cake. Remember that calories fuel your body with energy to ensure you maintain ample strength to achieve your goals while showcasing your best self.

As the cross-country season ended and snowdrifts disrupted long runs, my body reflected the pasty-pudge of bagels. Drowsily stumbling into the shower room one morning, I hung up my towel, turned on the water, reached for the curtain—and paused. Cheap lighting mixed with sunshine beaming through a window as I caught my nakedness in a large mirror ahead. Pale winter skin, flabby arms, stocky thighs, cascading belly rolls: was this really my body? As the sound of water streamed in my ears, I pushed and poked protruding flesh with cold fingers, as if testing dinner rolls for softness. Dead center my navel sat like a button on the cusp of bursting off a taut shirt. Twisting to see the worst, I stared at a white canvas displaying a wide purple birthmark textured with cottage-cheese indentations. Did this butt truly belong to me?

Latent fat aversions from childhood bubbled to the surface and erupted like a volcano: buxom family friends waiting with open arms for an embrace, a heavy-set Girl Scout leader waxing on about how to pitch Samoas to neighbors, and chubster couples at the Golden Corral buffet slyly dumping ribs and biscuits into purses for later. Now I was one of these people! I was a fat, greedy girl without self-control and the antithesis of a Sylvia; I was disgusting and did not deserve to be popular or cool. Cruising below initial superficial emotions, I hung my head in shame as I stepped into the shower.

Fat is a manifestation of my weakness—my greed and lack of control. This disgusting body is proof that I am not good enough and do not deserve praise.

I considered sprinting into the morning light, running for hundreds of miles until the fat melted from my body and the sun turned my stomach into a flat, bronze landscape. Already late for class, however, I furiously scrubbed my skin raw until anger gave way to powerful resolve. This was the last time I washed this pathetic body! I would not submit to fatness. I would turn the tide to prove my worthiness. I would rise into the heavens as a beautiful star, deserving of praise and love. Toweling off and scurrying down the hallway, I absorbed feelings of hope and confidence. Today was a new day and I would take advantage of it.

I walked down the cafeteria steps that evening with a steadfast heart. I was accustomed to cafeterias eliciting frightening emotions. There was now, however, a sinister and dangerous dimension: this was a battlefield pitting self-control against temptation. While my friends discussed spring break plans, I eyed the mashed potatoes with suspicion and questioned whether the chicken a la king or the turkey meatloaf was the lesser of the two evils. Passing by the dessert offerings while grasping a peach tray for support, I examined the cake slices. Taunting students atop white plates, these bakes now appeared as prostitutes, selling their white bleached bodies with fake dyes, cheap frostings, and revealing layers. Marching past their invitations, I sat down with my meatloaf and stared at the bagel dispenser across the room. How could I be so naive? Just yesterday I had accepted these circular symbols of gluttony as doughy friends! I had allowed memories of flipping Elephant Ears on warm summer nights and biting into jammy Berliner donuts to cloud my judgement. I knew better now.

Over the ensuing months, I invented lame reasons to avoid dinner with friends. Still compelled to prove I could survive an Ivy League education, dinner became an opportunity to complete transfer applications and to study for the ACT while enjoying "safe" turkey wraps. After years of aching for cafeteria acceptance, I was isolating to avoid food, a vital feature of humanity I'd loved since infancy. And yet, although I was preparing to combat hunger cues and avoid temptations, I was not ready to fully commit to skinny aspirations. My healthy self was still hanging on inside, championing self-love over self-hate. Consequently, as I crunched into a pickle and filled out application bubbles one evening, I hesitated. What was I doing? Finishing my dinner and closing my work, I raced back to my dorm, following the sounds of laughter until I arrived at the coziest room in the hall. Twisting open a Keebler sandwich as we coordinated schedules for a trip to the Jersey Shore, I rejoiced in my decision to be amongst friends and settled into the pleasure of chocolatey sweetness.

SELF-LOVE GEM: REACH OUTWARDS

You do not need to struggle alone in your physical and mental challenges with anorexia, bulimia, or any other debilitating force! Retreating inwards often appears like the best solution; we want to hide under our covers to be alone in our pain. Isolation, however, is a self-induced roadblock to health and happiness. Rather than permitting an inner voice to fill lonely places with destructive thoughts, reach out! There is no gold star for struggling alone; asking for support is a braver and wiser decision. Place your trust in friends, family, or licensed professionals that sincerely want to help you reach a safe place of well-being. With encouragement, you can work through underlying issues rather than using food as a negative coping mechanism. If I had confided in a university counselor or dietician at this point, I might have reconnected with my inherent worth, realized I am good enough, and enjoyed an easier life in the ensuing years.

6

BLINDLY HEADING INTO THE ED DESERT

PHILADELPHIA, PENNSYLVANIA: AGE 18

For a high-strung perfectionist, a UPenn acceptance was a blessing and a calamity. After a lifetime splashing about as a clever fish in a small pond, I became a minnow in a 300,000-gallon Oceanarium teeming with angel, butterfly, and betta fish that only intensified my desire for thinness. I might have reflected on the absurdity of comparing my thighs to those under the skirts of Penn's skinniest women. Instead, I dipped my toes into a whirlpool of binging in an irrational attempt to acquire a pair of stiletto-worthy Heidi Klum legs.

All of this danger, however, came later! At the outset, I arrived for orientation on a lofty cloud of excitement, optimism, and acceptance. As I mingled with a crowd of transfer students at the Jamaican Jerk Hut on trendy South Street, I thanked my stars for a strong enough ACT score to land a seat at this cheerful table. I was surrounded by an eclectic group of misfits —kids just like me who had lived around the world and were shaped by unique backgrounds. Suddenly it seemed normal that I called Oklahoma, Canada, and Nowhere "home" and grew up in a Mormon, Army family. Thrilled by this unexpected sense of belonging, I let my true colors fly free. At Penn, I would reveal my authentic, sporty self, noshing on mustard-laden dogs at Phillies games and dancing downtown until dawn without any restrictive inhibitions or social anxieties. Digging my spoon into a communal coconut cake, I exhaled an audible sigh of relief—maybe I was finally home.

I was still on a coconut cream high a few afternoons later when I arrived at the Registrar's office to defend my Art History transfer credits. As I drummed up the courage to do battle over the hours I'd spent memorizing artifacts like the titillating *Reclining Couple on a Sarcophagus*, my eyes suddenly alighted on a nearby menagerie. Layering this way and that in a large glass cookie jar, lions, tigers, and rhinos were waiting to be fished out with a large spoon resting inside. After confirming the coast was clear, I moved closer to the jar, lifted the lid and spoon, and dropped a few animals into a waiting hand. I bit into a tiger first; his light taste and smooth texture went down surprisingly easy. Maybe food like this could be trusted? Perhaps I did not need to be on my guard with *all* food, so long as it was clean and simple. Licking vanilla crumbs off my lips a few moments later, I concluded I could eat mini monkeys, camels, and tigers without feeling fat. As I contentedly sat back from my snack, the door opened and I gathered my confrontational powers to defend my Elizabethtown credits.

∼

Opting out of all cafeteria options on my housing application was liberating. After a quick introduction to a cake in our fridge by a cheerful, new roommate, "Please, help yourself! And that goes for the baked ziti on the lower rack!", I dashed across campus to seek safety in a local grocery store. The store was spanking new and brandished a Whole Foods vibe that was mind-blowingly modern in 2001. Slowing my pace, I felt like Dorothy arriving into the Emerald City while exploring wide aisles stocked with foodie treasures: bins loaded with nuts and granola mixes, fresh sandwiches and salads to-go, and fruits in attractive crates with signs proclaiming their origins. I wasn't sure whether it's best to be a horned melon from Africa or a Honeycrisp from a local farm, but the variety was stunning. As I headed to the checkout bearing yogurt, bananas, and cereal, my little eye spotted a container in the shape of a bear. It wasn't as elegant as the Registrar's jar, but the same crackers were packed inside by the hundreds. On a whim, this bear and I trotted home together.

A few hours later, I settled into my new digs to plow through a complicated

Thomas Hobbes reading assignment. A few paragraphs in, I twisted the lid on my new bear container to munch on a few animals. I read a few paragraphs and dipped back into the bear. With a container filled to capacity, what was one more handful? Turning the page, I looked back at the bear and decided to eat three or four more. Fast forward forty-five minutes and I understood nothing about Hobbes and a lot about how it feels to get sick off safari animals. It was a struggle to recollect what had happened. It was as if I'd entered an out-of-body state, completely detached from reality. Now here I was, staring at a bear missing half its occupants and over-whelmed by feelings of guilt and despair. I wanted to travel back in time to place the bear back on the shelf, or die: those seemed like my two best options. Physically shaking with shock, horror, and shame, I screwed the lid back on and relo-cated the bear on the highest shelf outside my room. As the ache in my belly continued, a thought flitted across my brain.

Why not try to stop eating? Not all at once; of course not! But eating less each day will ensure I feel calm and in control.

This simple thought aligned with my current trajectory. I was already accustomed to eating less at meals and choosing the salad option on dinners out with friends. But this was a loaded gun—permission to purposefully restrict. I would eventually realize an extension of my inner critic, my "eating disorder voice", had dropped this idea into my thoughts. It's hard to know when this voice first tiptoed into my mind. Was she there when I was ditched in high school? Was she observing my horror as I stared at exposed flesh in the shower mirror? Years later, I would call her out as a manipulative liar seeking to kill my happiness like the sorceress Maleficent. "Mal" saw in me a protégé; someone she could mold and protect from a world where only the skinny or beautiful can succeed. She was not concerned with my relationships, health, self-worth, or lasting happiness; rather, she demanded I be whipped and prodded to achieve her skinny aspirations. If mental breakdowns, malnutrition, and an early death were unintended consequences, so be it.

The minutes and hours ticked by as I struggled to refocus on Hobbes. As the wild animals in my belly settled and the clock struck late O'clock, my stomach began to growl. Scowling, I ignored its pleas and hunkered down to highlight passages until, too hungry to concentrate any longer, I stepped into the bathroom to brush animal remains out of my molars. As a curious Georgette, I might have stayed up to research how to create lean muscles without resorting to starvation. But it was too late; the idea of restricting was far more tantalizing than nutritional truth. Frankly, I didn't care what might happen to my bone density, brain, or organs if I denied myself over the years. Losing weight was my ultimate desire, and in my distorted world view, "food" and "thinness" are diametrically opposed forces. All food was villainess and, as clear as the Crystal Light in my cupboard, a low-calorie diet held the key to perfection. Consequently, rather than becoming an educated human, I fell asleep to the sound of unhappy grumbles.

SELF-LOVE GEM: SEEK HAPPINESS CENTERED GOALS

Creating a super skinny body is not a worthy goal! Instead of engaging in destructive behaviors, choose goals that will improve your overall well-being. I could have positively reacted to this experience by becoming a nutritional guru or learning how to prepare satisfying meals for my roommate and friends. Instead, I allowed an animal cracker incident to become a lynchpin for a destructive lifestyle. What meaningful and realistic goals can you set to challenge your demons and increase your happiness? Perhaps you'd like to start a garden to spend more time in the sunshine, or maybe enrolling in an Italian language course is your speed. Even if it's something as simple as starting each day with a positive affirmation, pursuing healthy goals can improve your mood and move you forward on your journey towards Recovery and joyful living.

My arms reached overhead with satisfaction; I'd slept through the night without breaking for food! The balloon in my stomach was gone, my animal cracker catastrophe was ancient history, and my mental and physical health were restored. After promptly dropping my half-empty bear container into a dumpster on the way to class, I plucked a banana out of my bag. As I merrily stripped its peel down and took a bite, a handful of Sylvias zigzagged across the center of campus. Today I was pledging their sorority as a to-be skinny chick; soon I would also exude confidence and grace, poise and beauty in short skirts, buttery leather jackets, and golden highlighted locks! I'd require a super-cute boyfriend, a rad internship, and a fulfilling volunteer role or two, but all of those details could be worked out later—once I was thin.

I continued to soar on an empty mental high until midway through a morning lecture when hunger pangs bombarded my belly. "Grrrrrorrororrrrrrrrrrugh!!!!" my stomach roared, demanding to be heard.

Not now, you greedy gut! You don't know what's best for me and can't be trusted. If I listen to you, I'll never reach perfection!

My belly didn't give a fig about thinness, of course. Rallying against my stubbornness, it furtively sounded the alarm for food until, my body crumbling under the pressure, I raced home and devoured two giant bowls of Basic 4 cereal. Once more sickly full and defeated as the bottom of my bowl appeared, I skipped dinner and vowed that tomorrow I would resist urges to eat. Unaccustomed to starvation, however, my willpower continued to crash over the ensuing weeks as I became trapped in a restrict-binge-restrict cycle. Sometimes I lasted until 4:00 p.m.; sometimes I broke at 11:00 a.m; sometimes I survived on 200 calories until noon; sometimes I inhaled a 10oz bag of M&Ms at 9:00 p.m. Unable to regulate, I created rules in a resolute attempt to stay on track:

- I will only eat once every eight hours
    - I will only consume cold, simple foods for lunch and breakfast
    - Dinner will include a protein and vegetables

. . .

I was certain I'd feel tremendously empowered living a restrictive existence with fixed parameters. I was on my way to becoming a happy, strong, and confident Sylvia with the world at my fingertips! As the months passed, however, and I continuously found myself at the bottom of a pack of M&Ms or a box of Cinnamon Pop-Tarts, I felt wretched. Riding back and forth on a seesaw of starvation and immense fullness, I lost faith and trust in myself.

Why am I so weak? Why is it so hard to stop eating? How can I be so greedy? Will I ever be good enough?

∿

A budding ED seriously interfered with university life. Half of my brain fixated at all times on a reel of negative thoughts that destroyed my peace and self-esteem. Hangry and weak, concentrating in lectures and stringing together irregular verbs in French was intolerably challenging. Apart from confiding to a best girlfriend about my battle for self-control, I struggled in silence. I may have intended to expose the real me at Penn, but that didn't need to include the awkward and shameful bits, right? In my mind, there was a fine line between skinny coolness and bulimic grossness; therefore, I subconsciously concluded, I must never admit to having a problem.

Even with food interference, however, I loved Penn! As would be the case throughout my twenties, spiritual escapes into nature and meaningful connections offset mental and physical torture. Whether releasing endorphins on marathon runs along the Schuylkill River, shaking my hips in smoky clubs to Eminem and Beyoncé, or raising the roof to Busta Rhymes at Penn's annual Spring Fling concert, present moments released my true self and filled my cup with positive vibes. I couldn't name a single Busta song, but it didn't matter—

I felt I belonged in Philadelphia and was uplifted by kindness, laughter, cool breezes, and the tranquility of the river. Consequently, when I finished university a semester early and moved to New York, I carried a vile eating disorder that would plague my soul for years, but I also left with pocketfuls of happy memories I held onto when times got tough.

7

ASPIRATIONS OF PURGING AND PASTA TWIRLING

NEW YORK, NEW YORK: AGE 21

I moved to Manhattan's Upper East Side to start a career in Public Relations. After applying for entry level positions at New York's top firms, I was jazzed to accept an offer as a CEO's and Vice President's shared executive assistant. I had no actual idea what the job entailed, but presumed it involved decorating offices with fresh cut flowers, shopping for the CEO's wife at Bergdorf Goodman, and providing the executive team with clever campaign launches. Essentially, I hoped to star in a romantic comedy. Here's what really happened...

∼

It was a beastly twenty degrees when I flew into JFK and the key to my apartment refused to turn. After an evening hunt to locate an open locksmith (my new roommate was still away on holiday), I realized $700 a month for rent did not include the Carrie Bradshaw city view I had anticipated. There was no balcony whatsoever and my room did not include a window or

45

a bed. After a few uncomfortable nights, I accepted a bed as a necessity and dialed 1-800 Mattress to score the cheapest twin on offer. Realizing my $30,000 job also wouldn't stretch as far as I thought, I recalibrated my decor expectations. Skipping out on a bed frame or any other seemingly unnecessary furniture, I lived eight inches from the floor for the rest of the year. I took heart that my surroundings exuded a minimalist, Japanese style of living.

The next morning, I wrapped up Eskimo style and bounded out of my windowless abode, brimming with nervous excitement. To my dismay, there were no fresh cut flowers or welcoming committee when I arrived at my office, located in the top section of a skyscraper in the heart of Times Square. There were, however, scores of Manhattan Sylvias racing by with crisp white stacks of papers and venti coffee cups; each one polished from end to end in cute A-line skirts, low-cut silk blouses, and sky high black heels. It was Boston preseason all over again, but with Louis Vuitton purses and covetable Tiffany & Co. charms. Noting that my wardrobe once again required burning, I announced myself at reception and was directed upstairs for training. After readjusting her black-rimmed glasses on a bulbous nose speckled with freckles, my trainer recalibrated my expectations: "You're here to manage the whim of two fat cats without question and to accept blunt feedback with stoicism and grace." At least that's what I heard. Wide-eyed with shock as she proceeded to run through their Outlook calendars, I considered interrupting to shout out truth.

Wait! Stop! I'm not the girl for this job! I'm forgetful with zero attention to detail and a bum that needs to move and groove!

But it was too late. I had a new twin mattress, an apartment on the Upper East Side, and a black roller chair ready for my butt to give it some TLC. As most of us do, I learned to sit for eight hours a day and to accept my entry level lot. I also learned to humor a vile Vice President who reeked of stale Vienna sausages and Italian vinaigrette mixed with Aqua de Gio cologne. Standing just over five feet, his stormy yellow eyes rolled around in his head like a disgruntled emoji face as he waxed on about his sexual exploits throughout the day. While I'm sure his nights involved more porn and booze than bombshells, my innocent mind was horrified. My hatred of the VP's licentiousness, smelly lunches, and erratic behavior was matched by a dread of the CEO, who ate assistants and analysts for breakfast. Although running at first light through Central Park's wooded trails calmed my worst jitters, I couldn't outrun the fear in my heart. Isolated and trapped, I arrived at work each morning shaky, unsettled, and ready to puke.

A love junkie in my heels would have fueled her body with energy boosting shakes, sandwiches, soups, and parfaits. She would have realized I deserved to feel valued, accepted, and appreciated, and hightailed it to the HR department to sort out her situation. Timid and naïve, I instead attempted to control my life by firing-up my ED. Two men might dominate my mind, but I would decide what enters my body! Unfortunately, practicing self-mastery usually meant starving myself throughout the day with only a large blueberry muffin for sustenance. I knew Manhattan's food truck muffins were laden with trans fats and sugars; chunky little devils manufactured to survive a nuclear disaster and rides down the sarcophagus of Times Square tourists. But, without a nutritional label or any strong flavors, muffins offered an easy diet solution until the late afternoon, when my esophagus hit a final faux berry and raised hell. As my belly cried for more, it became impossible to focus on the muddy colors of my Outlook calendar and to ignore the VP's smarmy comments.

By the day's end, I was a withered blueberry on a vine and

desperate to satiate the raw, aching hunger in my stomach. As I walked upwards into a winter wind at my subway stop and rounded the last block home, I'd catch a hint of rising dough emanating from the pizzeria underneath my building. Sometimes I'd resist and create a homemade salad loaded with chicken, croutons, and dill pickles. After the longest of days, however, I'd pull open the pizzeria's door to bask in the warmth of comforting aromas. After trading a ten-spot for a Diet Coke and a takeaway box, I'd rush upstairs to strip into a white tank and jeans before opening my cardboard treasure box. A quiet sanctuary, a chilled Coke, a copy of Steinbeck's *East of Eden*, and a folded-over cheese slice—what could be finer on a cold and lonely night? Drops of orange and yellow grease strained off-white pages as I'd find my place and nourish my starving body with swaths of mozzarella cheese. As I'd continue flipping pages while tackling slice after slice, I'd spiral into binge-mode, rereading the same paragraph until I was faced with the grim reality of an empty takeaway box, stained Steinbeck pages, and a fit-to-bust belly. Such dreadful episodes continued like a depressing, looped Radiohead song until Mal dropped a thought into my mind one night.

Why not puke it up? You can take back the pain! You can pretend tonight never happened.

Anxious but hopeful, I heeded this call to action. Conjuring up stereotypical images of prima ballerinas retching for the sake of ethereal leaps and pirouettes, I was prepared to become a skinny woman who excuses herself in restaurants to discreetly purge. I timidly knelt at the foot of my porcelain throne and took a breath. Then carefully, apprehensively, I extended a pointer finger into the recesses of my throat. Nothing. I cautiously inched my finger a bit further back, but still no luck. Furious at my overzealous gag reflex, I scratched my nail on the upper reaches of my throat until, wincing, tears emerged from my frightened eyes. I stood upright to stare at the empty bowl and lament my performance.

I can't properly starve myself or even puke up pizza! Can I do anything right at all? How am I so pathetic?

After locating the scrubber and giving the toilet a cleaning, I felt slightly better. Perhaps I was never meant to be bulimic; perhaps starving was a more respectable way to achieve thinness. Speculating that an outdoor cat lifestyle would spur a binge-free, skinny existence, I picked my greasy puddle off the floor, popped two antacids, and headed for the door, determined to never eat dinner at home alone again. Moonlight walks, usually with a "safe" sandwich in my mitts, became my nightly salvation. Tromping through sidewalk slush as Dido or The Black Eyed Peas jammed on my iPod mini, pervy bosses, faux blueberry muffins, cheap black heels, and binges fell by the wayside. Feelings of peace and security thawed my heart from the inside-out as I walked down 5th Avenue in the company of suited doormen and fellow New Yorkers also braving February's chill, temporarily liberated from a disorder I already hated more than anyone or anything.

The sighting of a beautiful Manhattanite occasionally interrupted my dreamy moonlight reveries. I once spotted an elegant woman through the frosted window of an Italian restaurant. She was dressed in a silky jade top and sparkly earrings, and clinking glasses with a handsome man across the table. As she smiled and readjusted her hair, I wondered if she was happy in her life. Was she as perfect as she seemed? Was she out with her husband while a nanny looked after their children? Or was she harboring fears, doubts, and maybe even a horrid disorder? Laughing merrily, she chatted with her date as she spun strands of angel hair on her fork and took small bites. Lingering an instant more, I watched as she continued her process of spinning and eating, vicariously feeling strands of fresh pasta in my mouth and the smooth taste of olive oil on my tongue. The more pasta she twirled, the better I felt. Here was proof a thin and seemingly ideal woman ate more than just salad.

Someday I'll twirl pasta across from a handsome man without the fear of eating too much. Once I'm in control of my body and mind, I'll create a lovely existence and radiate a binge-free happiness. Someday I will be good enough again.

SELF-LOVE GEM: REALIGN YOUR COMPARISONS

How often do comparisons work in your favor? Have you ever compared yourself to a supermodel to draw attention to your sexiness? Probably not! Usually, we measure ourselves against others to emphasize our inadequacies and to demonstrate how crap we are at managing our lives. Are your comparisons fair? Do you compare yourself on a Thursday afternoon to a flawlessly airbrushed Victoria Secret model? Do you weigh-up your layer cake against an Instagrammer who posts pics of her best bakes for a living? Don't be fooled —most of us show the world our highlight reel, and even the most glam celebrities have their rough moments! Consequently, how about appreciating the good in your life? What details (no matter how minor) can you love about yourself? Next time you're at a beach, pool, or gym and feel inclined to compare your body to the most stunning woman in sight, do yourself a favor: include all the other women in view into your sample. Chances are you'll feel a bit more grateful for the body you're lucky to own. And with practice, you might simply know (without glancing at the others) that you are wonderful, just as you are.

8

FEARFUL ISOLATION TO SWEET LIBERATION

WEINAN, CHINA: AGE 22

I realized I was moving to China when I woke up at 35,000 feet to the foul odor of kimchi. Fumbling for a barf bag as my gut retched with horror, I willed the plane to turn around immediately. Once again, however, it was too late: Air China Flight 888 was somewhere over the Pacific and I was expected in Xi'an that morning. There was a method to my mad decision to move to China. Moonlight escapades were marvelous and, as spring erupted in Central Park, New York transformed into a utopia of sunbathers, Mr. Softee ice cream trucks, and free outdoor concerts. Tulips and soft-serve, however, could not overcome the reality of horrible bosses and a muffin diet existence. No matter how hard I willed myself to hunker down until I transformed into a pasta twirling Manhattanite, I could not. Consequently, when my brother Shawn suggested I quit and apply to British History programs abroad, I leapt at the opportunity. I hated the idea of running away, but sometimes, I told myself, a girl has to flee from something toxic to discover something sweet and groovy. Slipping applications in the mail, I wondered if teaching abroad might be a productive way to pass the time before (fingers crossed) starting grad school. Prowling Google, I stumbled upon Aston English, an American company opening a school in a remote Chinese village called Weinan. Romantically envisioning myself in a *Crouching Tiger, Hidden Dragon* setting, I signed up and hoped for the best.

I rendezvoused with my Chinese driver at the Xi'an Airport and soon we were speeding through a somber landscape at odds with the vivid forests and flowering jasmine I'd envisioned. Winter would eventually break its hold on China, but this was the height of midwinter before Chinese New Year brought the promise of spring. As we drove past quiet villages and clusters of huts tucked into steep hillsides, I wondered if China's notorious dictator Mao was behind these humble habitations. I also wondered if he was behind sour smelling kimchi, since who in their right mind would encourage people to eat this for breakfast when Captain Crunch or simply toast was available? I would later learn that kimchi was developed in Korea and that it is terribly good for your health. Fermented foods didn't appear on the 1980s food pyramid, however, and, again, I didn't care a fig about nutrition.

Our little bug car came to a halt an hour later. Weary from traveling, I cautiously stepped out to assess my surroundings. Grey dirt circled everywhere, combining with my driver's cigarette drags and the smoke of nearby coal fires to create a gloomy haze. In stark opposition to all this cheerlessness, my eyes spotted a display of bold colors across the street. A large Mongolian woman was posted up beside red, blue and green plastic buckets. Catching my stare, she returned my gaze with a similar fascination. She blinked first, which set off a chain reaction of her laughing merrily and reshuffling her buckets, which

I'd soon discover held mountains of bean sprouts, the province's humble culinary hero. After smiling back at this unknown woman, I turned back towards my driver. Flicking his cig butt on the dusty earth, he escorted me to a tidy apartment that was simply decorated but included a Queen size bed topped with a fluffy duvet. Cozying up in jelly roll style, I nestled in and took a nap.

A heavy knock disrupted my jelly roll siesta. Two men stood at the door; one was a lanky Australian wearing a New York Yankees wool hat that looked very silly on his head. Introducing himself as Aston's regional manager, he explained he was in town to liaison with Max, the gentleman at his side and the school's Chinese franchise owner. I immediately loved Max, a Weinan local in his forties whose mirth and laughter transcended our cultural divide. After verifying my fridge was stocked with the oranges and hard boiled eggs he'd arranged, Max raised his arms and announced in broken English, "We celebrate you now! We go to lunch; very good."

There's nothing more delightful than a free lunch—except when you're deep inside an eating disorder and every calorie is meticulously examined. After two years of dodging expected food hazards, my time was up; today I would be forced to eat like a "normal" person. I was soon shaking hands with Max's wife and his Chinese school staff in a beautifully decorated restaurant. In stark opposition to the bleak countryside, wall hangings, tablecloths, and painted vases reflected the bright red and gold of the Chinese flag. As we waited for lunch to appear on a massive circular table, I weakly attempted small talk with my neighbors while my thoughts centered on a silently waiting lazy Susan ahead.

What can I expect? How much do I need to eat so people don't know I have a problem? Will all of the food be hot? Will there be kimchi? I can say no to anything! It's my body and I will not be taken advantage of!

When the food did appear, I smiled with relief—this was a meal of lightly dressed vegetables, noodles, and individual soups. Thanking heaven above, I helped myself to a small portion of each and every dish and, after enjoying seconds of the chilled leeks for good measure, I sat back with satisfaction. Yes, I was overly full and wasn't crazy about a generous dousing of vinegar on seemingly everything, but I was unquestionably victorious! Just then, however, a server arrived bearing a platter releasing graceful clouds of hot steam. I furled my brows for a moment, puzzled, until I realized the worst: we had only eaten the appetizers. My mood tanked like an elevator with a broken cable hurtling downwards. Manic thoughts jumbled with colorful expletives while I choked back angry tears and attempted to keep my cool.

How could they do this to me on my very first day? Why am I even here? I don't belong here! I want to return to my bananas and blueberry muffins! Get me out of here!

Without an escape, I polished my chopsticks against each other and launched into a plentiful second course as dishes continued to appear at our table. I attempted to detach my mind from my body as I took hit after hit, willing myself to continue on until the lazy Susan stopped her dance and every chopstick lay still. I felt senseless and stupefied on the drive home, as if attempting to process a violation on my body. As Max's little Chinese car dropped me off, the regional manager called out, "We'll swing by again to pick you up at 7:00 p.m. for dinner!" Minutes later, as a tightening in my throat and lungs combined with a heavy ache in my heart, I consoled myself in the arms of my duvet, allowing tears to stream uncontrollably down my face. The physical and emotional pain hurt so bad, and yet I was expected to eat again in a matter of hours. How could I endure it?

Max's generosity knew no bounds. Week after week, he showcased his appreciation to the Aston crew by hosting daily feasts. With Mal dropping food guilt and starvation tactics into my mind, however, I reduced my intake as much as possible. Skipping breakfast every morning, I arrived at lazy Susans prepared to face a poached, boiled, or steamed fish and a roasted duck with plum sauce and pancakes. I became adept at shuffling pieces of rice and meat about with my chopsticks, lifting morsels up to my mouth and then bringing them quickly down to tap on my pod of rice. A stealth table ninja, I avoided carbs, heavy creams, and pasta dishes, skipping bites of rice here, and avoiding an extra helping of chicken there. After dinners, Max invited us to sip on green tea at one of his exquisite tea shops decorated with richly painted calligraphy, koi fish, and slender, white birds. Simple tall glasses filled with boiling water defied my belief that hot water shatters glass as a server gingerly rested a few leaves on top. After consuming copious amounts of food, I was struck by the delicacy of these leaves. Simple, calm, elegant, lithe: I wished to mirror their existence by silently floating on clean water without any food angst to disturb my peace.

～

I was settled into teaching and charmed by my smallest students who eagerly selected sweet English names like "Joy", "Amelia" and "Cookie". With a continuous round of feasts paired with the onset of an intestinal disease, however, I was far from resembling floating tea leaves. Rather, I often resembled a porcupine, rolled up on my duvet as oppressive cramps seized the sides and middle of my belly. I was quick to blame not just the local Szechuan spice, but food in general. The proof was in the rice pudding! Oils, rice, noodles, and vegetables could not be trusted and now, after an endless stream of Max Meals, I would die of digestive failure without biting into one last American Chocolate-Chip Cookie. Before completely giving into this tragic fate, however, I rang Max for help and within the hour we were driving to Xi'an's main hospital with Crystal, his English translator, in tow.

The arrival of a sick blonde in the hospital's Gastro wing caused a minor sensation. A young, attractive doctor with experience in a Boston hospital communicated his intentions. "I will investigate your stomach. We will send a little camera into your mouth and down to see more clearly. You will be brave." Discovering this was an anesthetic-free situation, I threw back a shot of a murky liquid Crystal handed over. "Take for the great pain this will make," she advised with a sympathetic look. As a crowd of men in lab coats filed into the room to watch, the doctor ensured I was sitting with a straight back. Then, tilting my head backwards, he lowered the tube down my throat. Like any self-respecting foreigner undergoing an operation thousands of miles from home, I gritted my teeth and silently howled for my mom. In a sudden show of kindness, Crystal squeezed my shaking hand and pressed her other hand onto my knee. Down, down, down the camera descended as I watched the monitor and a dozen eyes in my peripheral vision. "Nearly there," the doctor encouraged. As I felt the scratch of the tube and tears blur my vision, I deliriously considered my situation. I was a hopeless purger, but when called upon, I was ace at keeping it together for a foreign object to wander into my bowels! I might have laughed at this absurdity if a tube wasn't blocking my larynx. When the camera at last popped back up, I inhaled deep breaths of unobstructed air and waited for the verdict. The ins and outs of an intestinal disease didn't translate well into English, but I happily committed to swallowing a shopping bag full of every-color-of-the-rainbow pills. At the insistence of the doctor, I also swore to stop eating spicy and oily foods; a vow I accepted with pleasure.

While I dutifully threw back pills, Max occasionally stopped by my apartment with my favorite honey and walnut "Jiaozi". Dumplings are the pizza of China. Like our western version, these mini pockets run the gamut of street food to posh appetizers and are best experienced in dumpling joints, where servers race about with stacks of bamboo steamers stuffed with pork, shrimp, beef, and mixed vegetables. A dumpling joint lunch with Max was a frightful experience due to the volume of dough one must consume to reach the fillings. Dumplings, however, are exceptionally neat and clean; a safe option after the glitz and glammy eats on Weinan's restaurant platters. Consequently, after I got sick and Max Meals tapered off, Jiaozi became my cooking inspiration. Although I often boiled the stuffings out of my packaged grocery store varieties, I grinned with satisfaction as I sat down to a steaming bowl each night. Alone with dumplings and a few street DVDs, I expected to shed my Max Meals weight in no time.

This was far from the case! Not only was I far less vigilant about my portions, but, per usual, isolating was a conduit to binging. Stricken by familiar compulsions to eat at full tilt, I tossed aside chopsticks to cruise through dozens of dumplings with a sturdy fork before finishing off the night with a pack of Oreos, curiously sold everywhere in China. After one colossal feast, I awoke to discover a massacre from the previous night: fallen chopsticks, a large, sticky white bowl with black streaks, and a telltale empty roll of Oreos crumbs. Horrified by my truth, I realized I could no longer blame Max Meals or spicy foods for my troubles.

I am a fat girl without self-control! I cannot be trusted. I am a weak glutton who does not deserve to be loved. I will never be good enough.

Hanging my head with shame as I absorbed Mal's words, I wondered how I could continue on thousands of miles away from my family and friends.

∾

Aston's enrollment was doubling. This meant the arrival of Sarah, an Irish girl my age with teaching experience and decent Mandarin skills. Riding in on a cool April breeze as a tall and peppy Mary Poppins, Norin's blue eyes danced with amusement over cultural confusions and the unexpected challenges of living in remote China. Lively conversation and zestful laughter transformed my gray skies into a palette of vibrant colors. Together we travelled thousands of miles by train to raft on the Yellow River, follow Marco Polo's Silk Road atop smelly camels, and splurge on a posh hotel on the desert's edge to cool our sunburnt bodies under crisp, cotton sheets. More than an adventure companion, Sarah's arrival meant safety from binging as we explored freshly pulled noodles at hole-in-the-wall cafes, street donuts bobbing in steaming cups of soy milk, and various meats sizzling in boiling pots of oil, garlic, and cilantro.

As a special treat one afternoon, we caught the bus to Xi'an in search of pure gold: Chocolate Croissants. After wandering down wide streets and a maze of alleys, we entered a western market, making our way past boxes of Lucky Charms, Walkers Shortbread, and European chocolates until we sighted a counter displaying two silver trays of perfectly-shaped croissants. I couldn't understand why or how these beauties were here, but it didn't matter. Whether by magic or an enterprising Chinese baker in the back of the market, I was simply grateful.

After paying a shopgirl to hold a golden beauty in my fingers, I slowly bit into crunchy pastry. A strong smell of butter hit my nose as my teeth inched their way past flaky layers and airy pastry towards the chocolate center. Ooh La La! The taste overwhelmed my body with feelings of home, peace, and comfort. Suddenly Mal was silent and all the useless chatter in my mind dissolved; in this make-shift patisserie, there was only space to reconnect with a love of food I'd repressed for years. Christmas cookies, Rocky Road scoops, Elephant Ears, jammy Berliner donuts, and frosted birthday cupcakes—sugary childhood memories flooded back like a warm hug as I reached a final bite and joyfully swallowed it down. After sweeping any last crumbs off our plates, Sarah and I retraced our steps back onto Xi'an's busy streets. Although the usual smells of coal, smoke, and frying oils perfumed the air, today I was cocooned in buttery nostalgia and impervious to my foreign environment. Whereas isolation was a speeding train to binging, in the company of a friend—if only for a few minutes—food was once more a sweet part of life.

SELF-LOVE GEM: RESTORE TRUST WITH FOOD

One of anorexia's worst features is coercing its victims to deny their instincts. We tell ourselves "I don't need food! I'm just as satisfied drinking meal replacement shakes than enjoying a varied assortment of fruits, veg, grains, and proteins." The truth, however, is that food is a vital aspect of being human and a glorious part of our life experience. Food is not your enemy. Rather, it is something to appreciate and savor, without fear, guilt, or restrictions. Whether you view cupcakes or fries as your mortal enemy, or find it challenging to bite into anything today, know that you deserve to eat, and to eat well! I would encourage you to take a leap of faith—stop into a bakery or burger joint to reconnect with something you love, or did once. Taste each bite, fully experiencing the textures and smells, while channeling gratitude for a body that sustains and supports your life.

SECTION III: STEPPING ONTO A TIGHTROPE

9

WE ARE NEVER GETTING BACK TOGETHER

LONDON, ENGLAND: AGE 22

C ozy pubs, flawlessly curated boutiques, and churches flaunting fancy spires create pockets of charm throughout London. On chilly afternoons, tucked away cafes offer an extra dose of sweetness as baristas prep frothy drinks to thaw cold fingers while customers bite into hefty scones slathered in jam. My first forays into London's heart included autumn runs through Hyde Park, the ideal place to watch silky hounds leap into the air for balls. Paired with the scent of dew and soft lavender, runs absorbed the last remnants of Xi'an's smoky smells in my system and released anxiety permeating through my body. It was October and I was in the thick of my graduate history program at the University College London. Already hypnotized by London's beauty and culture, I planned to stay forever as a professor who twirls pasta in London's chicest restaurants.

I had a knack, however, of making lemons out of a chilled glass of refreshing British lemonade. Once floods of women arrived on campus, I transformed from Vibrant American into

Terrified Rabbit, comparing my Gap conservatism to every chic Sylvia in sight. Trendy women were everywhere, channeling Sienna Miller in boho-chic tops and low-slung belts, rocking edgy looks in cropped leather jackets and short skirts, and racing out of cafes with men and oversized purses on their arms. My intimidation bled into my course lectures where bookish peers effortlessly swirled their tea while recounting the French Revolution. Ashamed by my physical and mental deficiencies, I left cocktail parties early, crumpled-up activity flyers, and entertained Mal's poisonous perspective on brisk morning walks to campus.

I'm already hungry. Did I finish that article for class? Can I say anything clever about it? Does it really matter—they all think I'm ridiculous already! Ugh, stop it stomach. I could get one of those apricot flapjacks bars... wait, no way rosé! It's not even 10:00 a.m., you greedy piggy!

That guy just looked at me. Is something wrong with my hair? Is it my thighs? It's definitely my thighs. These jeans aren't helping; why did I buy such stupid jeans? I can't be trusted with money; every decision I make is wrong. I spend too much money and eat too much food.

Can I pop into the store for a Diet Coke to take the edge off my hunger? I shouldn't be hungry; I ate way too much last night. Why did I eat so much? I should have skipped the rice; the chicken tikka was more than enough. I have no control, which is why my thighs are so big. I'm a greedy pig. Today I will try harder! I'll make sure everything I eat could fit onto one small plate.

I wasn't a completely tragic case; my true self sparkled and danced when given half a chance! Consequently, sunshine filled my wintry soul as I explored London's colorful neighborhoods, bantered in heels on an occasional date out, and set off on weekend expeditions with a small clique of American girls. Food got in the way, of course—keeping calm as friends passed around British Digestive cookies or a date unexpectedly ordered a crème brûlée and lemon tart for us to share was strenuous. With my true self cheering me onwards, however, brief pops of joy kept my boat afloat between destructive thoughts and bleak moments.

A bleak moment arose one March evening as I walked into Topshop's flagship store on Oxford Street. Having just survived an oral French exam, I felt entitled to a bit of retail therapy on my way home. I was also prepared to spend three purple £20.00 notes ($35.00 in 2006, nicked from my food budget) on something fun and flirty. Riding Topshop's elevator down three floors of UK trendiness, I played dress-up in wide-brimmed hats and five-inch heels, blingy sunglasses, glittery tops, and delicate lacy bras. Although not the statement pieces I'd envisioned, I eventually settled on a sleek black tank and pink ballet flats. Pleased with my purchases, I waltzed out of the store and down the Oxford Circus subway steps in pursuit of pizza and a good nights' sleep. Yes, that's right, pizza! I'd recently binged on Digestive cookies—and sworn them off forever—but tonight would be different. Tonight I would master the art of eating for one in the company of a cheese pie, an old friend I'd avoided and feared since living in Manhattan. Besides, it was after 7:00 p.m., my limbs were shaky after a day of Diet Coke and flapjacks (buttery granola bars), and I still had £15 to spare.

I was salivating with cheesy anticipation when I arrived home. After quickly changing into a white tank, jeans, and my pretty pink flats, I sat cross-legged on my floor and gave my cardboard companion and a Diet Coke my full attention. I eagerly popped open my soda and inhaled a few gulps before slowly and deliberately opening the box. Sweet heaven it smelled good! Immersing myself in its savory warmth, I released the largest slice from its family. Half; I would eat half —half was the right amount for a cool, composed, and collected Sylvia to eat. Once I bit in, however, I was overwhelmed by all-consuming urges to immediately continue onwards. Like a starved rabbit facing the cream-of-the-crop carrot, I noshed without breaking; chewing and swallowing saucy cheese and seasoned dough at a manic pace. When at last I came up for air, all that remained was an empty box and the greasy outline of eight missing slices.

My senses returned to my room: it was cold, silent and dimly lit. Why had I done it? Did I honestly believe I'd changed? Standing up to flop cheek-down on my green duvet, I accepted the truth of my crime and all my wretched feels. No, I could never be trusted alone with pizza, ice cream, cookies, or any of my "binge foods". Moreover, something had to give. I would rather die than continue on with an endless stream of hungry days sporadically topped off with horrific binges.

No more; I can't take it anymore!—I cried to the universe as tears flooded my pillow.

This will never happen again. Do you hear me pizza and cookies, ice cream and chips? We are never ever binging together. Ever.

I believed my Taylor Swift lyrical quote and can honestly say I've never binged since. I've eaten a lot now and again, but when I reach that "stop now or pass the point of no return" bridge, I stop. It's non-negotiable; as deep rooted as my vows to never shop at Costco on a Saturday or to wear Uggs in public. This might sound tremendously healthy and progressive; here was a chance to live a binge-free lifestyle. Unfortunately, however, I was simply "symptom switching" from bulimia to anorexia; a move that came with dangerous consequences. Binging on pizza or cookies was a heart-wrenching affair, but such episodes provided a stockpile of calories for my body to absorb when running on empty. Now that this safety net was removed, I became a candidate for hospitalization, or worse. Mal was elated by this turn of events. She knew I needed and trusted her now more than ever. With her commands and admonitions, we could "ride urges", overcoming physical pressures to eat for eight hours at a time until it was safe to consume a specific amount of food. Clinging onto my disorder for safety and strength as I pitched out the box, I hoped to once and for all become a skinny woman who is in control and worthy of praise.

SELF-LOVE GEM: EMBRACE YOUR BODY

I recently passed a beautiful woman who was running at a quick pace with a smile on her lips. I was so magnetized by her joyful spirit that I almost missed noticing she was exercising with a prosthetic leg. A humbling moment for sure, but also an inspiring one. Rather than zoning in on your imperfections, can you focus on how your body has supported you throughout your life? You might recall the rivers it's helped you to navigate, the degrees it has helped you to earn, the summer concerts it's allowed you to hear, and all the complex tasks—like breathing—it effortlessly handles. By practicing gratitude, you might start to appreciate those thighs you hate and begin to radiate loving kindness from the outside back in.

As London showers awoke spring flowers, writing a final dissertation at The British Library presented an ideal opportunity to perfect restrictive habits. With a naked flapjack bar in hand and a laptop in my purse, I'd walk through the library's imposing red brick and glass entrance each morning, climbing an elegant, modern staircase to a large and silent reading room. Once seated with a stack of dusty books, I'd type pages of notes into the afternoon, breaking only once to inhale another flapjack, a banana, and a Diet Coke.

An emancipated love junkie could have achieved as much or more this term. Her body rested and her mind free of a destructive voice, she would have worked in short blocks, taking occasional Kit-Kat and fresh air breaks to revive her body and senses. Chilled-out and maximizing her brainpower, she would have enjoyed the writing experience and left by sunset in pursuit of evening adventures. Deep inside an eating disorder, I instead reentered the world each night in an emotional daze, shattered yet devoted to a grim existence. I believed the pleasures of the outside world paled in comparison to the feelings of achievement I would experience as a skinny woman with a giant gold star on my work. Moreover, post pizza incident I found the stark reading room soothing, and the absence of visible food comforting. The faster I typed, the longer I sat, the less I ate, and the later I left, the stronger I felt. Finally I was living a binge-free lifestyle; transforming into a perfect woman with an idyllic body! In reality, however, I was locked in a mental prison built out of fear. Anxious I might lose control and "fail" on a food or academic front, I allowed rigid confinement to deprive my true self of health, connection, peace, and happiness.

Luckily, I retained a sense of normalcy via sporadic excursions with girlfriends and, even more auspiciously, once summer roses and rooftop bars reopened to reveal their aromas and charm throughout the city, I was forced to abandon my crazed lifestyle. Receiving a B- on my dissertation, along with a PhD application rejection, I left London without a skinny silhouette, a sexy British husband, a flock of university friends, or a Sienna Miller wardrobe. Although the experience felt like a failure, hindsight would eventually transform defeat into a lucky break. Saved from a solitary library sentence and a starvation diet of flapjacks and Diet Coke, I flew home to enjoy an endless summer in the safety of love, nature, and nutritious eats.

10

A MIDSUMMER'S DREAM & ROCK AND ROLL THINGS

LOS ANGELES, CALIFORNIA: AGE 23

My parents were living an hour outside of La La Land when I arrived on their doorstep without a plan. Fortunately, Brandon was also shacking-up at our family base to record a rock album without social distractions. Drawn to his rockstar dreams (and with twenty years of piano experience), I petitioned to become his musical collaborator. His enthusiastic consent resulted in us recording music and lyrics over a few idyllic months together. After blasting KT Tunstall's "Suddenly I See" as a morning wake-up call, we'd start laying tracks until it felt time to kick the soccer ball around at a nearby field, or to go on a taro boba run. Loaded with tapioca pearls that shot up our straws like schools of black pufferfish, an afternoon boba was a quick route to happiness, especially considering that taro tastes like my gram's Dansk pretzel-shaped cookies. Reconnecting to the piano as my vocal cords ran up octaves to test out verses, I reopened a channel to my soul. My true self saw the coast was clear to sing and dance, laugh and play. I'd spent a year convinced I was a serious academic destined to rent modern lofts in tiny urban spaces. Now I reevaluated this supposition. Releasing my creative side while communing with my spirit was euphoric; I felt more alive than I had in years. Consequently, rather than fantasizing about a history position at a northeast college, I daydreamed about becoming a singer-songwriter, as girls living around LA often do.

Ventures through Yosemite and Sequoia State Park with our parents added an extra layer of loveliness to this spiritual awakening. Coastal pines released perfumed smells of vanilla and butterscotch that elicited happy memories of traipsing through snowy mountains as a child. Waking up early to California's finest smells, I'd apprehensively bite into toasty Cherry Pop-Tarts before trekking through warm trails. While I mitigated fruit snacks and cookie breaks by discarding sections of sandwiches, munching in nature with my people was therapeutic. On the other side of the world from The British Library, parents transitioned into supportive friends and Brandon became a loyal wingman I could rely on for advice and friendship.

SELF-LOVE GEM: NOURISH YOUR SPIRIT

Regardless of its nature, spirituality is an essential component of our well-being that strengthens us in a myriad of unseen ways. Rather than an inconsequential break, jumping into waves or singing in a choir might be one of the most important activities of your week. Just as nourishing our bodies enables us to achieve small feats each day, a regular dose of spirituality lightens our load, releases peaceful feelings, and empowers us to weather storms when life gets gnarly. Whether dance, prayer, singing, meditation, or staring at the ocean is your jam, take time to nurture your spiritual side to reap the benefits of calm and uplifted spirits.

I wished the summer could last forever. As cool breezes swept through my ponytail on long distance runs, however, feelings of easy happiness collided with urges to achieve results in another brave new world. If Brandon and I created a minor sensation on the LA music scene, I could certainly cross into "good enough" territory by attaining the perfection I craved. Blinded by ambitious optimism, we rented an apartment in a sketchy part of Koreatown near downtown LA. Throwing open freshly washed windows to air out a lingering scent of paint, I welcomed a new beginning—until I was distracted by a disturbed man on the street below hollering at the world. I wasn't fazed. Our downtown skyline was magnificent and there was a Jacuzzi downstairs with little white fairy lights hanging overhead that make any place feel magical.

Even more enchanting were early autumn Shakespeare in the Park nights at Barnsdall Park, a hill dotted with olive trees overlooking Griffith Park. Swinging by KFC for a winner, winner chicken dinner en route, we'd smooth a blanket on thick grass and enjoy al fresco dining before the performance began. Fellow picnickers with their stemmed glassware and charcuterie spreads of cheeses, crostinis, pesto, jams and honey looked in dismay as we stuck our sporks into mashed potatoes. I suspected, however, that many of these folks were secretly envious of our finger lickin' spread and would happily trade their cured meats for our deep-fried drumsticks. As dusk fell we'd pull on our coats to listen to King Theseus declare "...how slow this old moon wanes!" Watching *A Midsummer Night's Dream* in the moon's soft glow was dreamy entertainment. Zipping my coat up to the very tip top, I'd breathe life into my cold hands while my soul hung onto every monologue, playful verse between fairies, and mischievous glances between lovers.

Most nights were less Shakespearean and more rock and roll as we jammed at a small studio in Hollywood with a couple of Italian musicians who wanted in on our national tour plans. Painting myself with thick layers of eyeliner and deep lipstick hues, I set my inner exhibitionist free in bedazzled skirts and tops, hoop earrings and headbands. Food rumination melted away as my fingers danced across the keys, passionately swaying and moving as my true self danced at the center of my heart.

I relished the thrill of living a double-life, but over the course of the year a daily grind dwarfed blissful evening happenings. I would eventually discover my spirit requires balance and that I cannot sustain a life infused with venomous people and an unrelenting ED voice, no matter how sparkly the lights or tasty the chicken. At the time, however, the ends appeared to justify the means. Come September the means included accepting an executive assistant position I knew I would hate ten minutes into the interview.

"How are you with difficult personalities? How are you under pressure? Give a recent example of how you cooled a heated situation," a no-nonsense woman in her early thirties commanded.

Ugh; I hate difficult personalities, confrontations, high stress environments, and unexpected chaos! I can't imagine anything worse than working for your boss! With rent dollars and band equipment to consider, however, I lied emphatically.

"I was born to deflate tense passions and situations! I prefer blunt, honest feedback and am available 24/7 to support a hustling executive."

I soon recalled why I hate assisting men who are twats, to borrow an apt British expression for stupid and obnoxious men.

Although less pervy than my New York boss, this one's temper was mightier. Impassioned midnight threats to fire me when a driver in the Middle East failed to appear or a Parisian hotel inexcusably closed their gym for renovations matched his raised voice and cutting remarks in the office. After particularly beastly confrontations, I'd find a quiet spot en route to the bus stop to have a good cry before catching the 720 Express home. Speeding through Beverly Hills and Koreatown, my pain ran deep as my anxiety settled along the journey. Attempting to ignore the stench of ripe body odor, stale fried foods, and auto repair grease permeating throughout the bus, I'd remove a bookmark from Tolstoy's *Anna Karenina* to lose myself in another woman's troubles. What an opportunity for an emancipated love junkie! Confidently aware of her innate value, she would have showered herself with such loving kindness:

I deserve to be treated with respect; I am not defined by a deplorable job and my boss is projecting his insecurities onto me! I am trying my best and I am good enough.

I'm sure she would have explained her needs to her boss or HR the following day, or reconnected to recruiters to secure a safe and positive situation.

Instead, a frightful reality spurred a revival of my ED as a coping mechanism. The discovery of Zone Bars in the lobby's convenience shop revitalized the restrictive torment of my British Library days. Zone Bars taste strongly of chemicals but at 190 calories each and packed with protein, two satiated my belly for twelve daylight hours—at least that was my ambition. Occasionally I broke with hunger, supplementing these "meals" with Diet Coke, Hershey Kisses, or a bag of fat-free popcorn before slinking home like a human test tube. Famished, I'd whip up dinner as quickly as possible so I could stretch out in a white tank and jeans beside Brandon as we devoured something substantial. After an initial race to line my gut, I'd leisurely taste each morsel, drawing out the juicy chew of chicken or smelling butter-fried mushrooms on my fork before swallowing. The pleasure of savoring food and feeling it travel through my system was sublime. Although I was inevitably plagued by regret after eating "too much", an injection of calories in my brother's good company calmed my nerves and satiated the raw ache in my belly.

SELF-LOVE GEM: RUN ON PREMIUM FUEL

Internalizing food solely in numeric calories terms is a limited perspective! Can you imagine if your body was transparent and you could see the impact of your choices? What if you could watch nutrients cruising into your brain to improve your mood? Surely you'd fill your body with the highest grade fuel possible and relinquish calorie counting! We operate best when our bellies are full of slow-burning, complex carbs, proteins, and fats. This doesn't mean skipping Friday night pizza or scraping the chocolate glaze off your donut. It means treating yourself with the consideration and respect you deserve: adding an extra tablespoon of peanut butter to your smoothie, snacking on fruits and nuts in the afternoon, or topping your breakfast cereal off with banana slices. Healthy doesn't mean boring; rather, it means loading up on a variety of textures and flavors that will keep you feeling calm and strong from the inside out.

Warm, full, and exhausted, Brandon and I rallied our energies to propel our rock tour aspirations forward. Although late night sessions with our band was a fab way to bang out frustrations, however, our main efforts were thwarted. Various industry contacts repeatedly proved to be all talk or terrible people, and attempts to fund our music ambitions through the stock market went from genius levels of success over months of trading to disastrous one fateful afternoon. I sobbed on the kitchen floor the moment I realized we were completely broke and that our upcoming tour was now kaput. I longed to press the restart button and reappear at my parents' house sipping a taro boba and heading out on a hike. If only I could reverse the tide of a stinky commute, a twat boss, a cruel eating disorder, and the grimy underbelly of Hollywood.

Shattered, Brandon and I hiked to the top of Griffith Park to reconsider our futures. Low on funds and working for an abusive man I couldn't respect, I confided to Brandon my desire to pursue happiness in a different place. A moment of inspiration descended as the sun began to fall behind an array of palm trees overlooking the city below. We had spent so many holidays at our grandparents' beach town outside of Vancouver and our gram was frequently voicing her loneliness. Vancouver was the mysterious city of my childhood, revealing its secrets to older cousins while I stayed back to watch Cinderella with a blackberry milkshake. Here was a chance to explore the hippest place in my imagination while satisfying a desire for geographical connection. What if I offered our gram companionship in exchange for a twin bed while Brandon closed up shop in Los Angeles and considered his next move? It was running away perhaps, but a split second decision to start over again seemed normal. Squeezing all my belongings into a suitcase *was* my normal and, unlike most people, evoked excitement and adventure, rather than fear and separation, in my heart.

I believed my only real loss was releasing a dream to follow in the footsteps of Sarah McLachlan, Alicia Keys, and other women who transform keyboards into a gorgeous extension of themselves. Communing with the piano was heavenly. Feeling the weight of the keys as my fingers moved in patterns was more than therapy—it was a joyful liberation of my true self. Consequently, small parts of my heart fractured as we auctioned off mics and guitars on eBay to strangers and locked up our studio one last time. Although my musician ambitions were short-lived, however, in the future I would look back fondly on the summer days we'd breathed in California pines while creating an album we loved. A twinge of relief mixed with excitement as I prepared to leave. Perhaps in Vancouver I could create a bright existence for my gram and me. Perhaps there I would find a way to be good enough; to be perfectly in control and skinny. Perhaps. As the sun dipped behind the palm trees swiftly turning into shadowed figures, we headed down the trail to feed our tired bodies with toasty Quiznos sandwiches.

11

A FLEETING, PYRRHIC VICTORY
VANCOUVER, CANADA: AGE 25

My Canadian Mountie grandpa had passed on to heaven's blackberry fields two years before. My gram, on the other hand, after decades of juicing beets and eating plain yogurt with seaweed, was a pillar of vitality. Now a zesty ninety-three-year-old woman with luminous skin and zero signs of brain deterioration, she became furiously indignant when neighbors applauded her age. "A woman's age is nothing to get excited about!" she'd proudly declare. Within minutes of knocking on my gram's house and running up her front steps for a squeeze, I was in the kitchen opening a cookie tin to ascertain what treats were sequestered therein. Disappointedly, bran muffins, not chocolate-chip cookies, were on offer that week, and I closed the lid as my gram cheerfully chatted about this and that arrangement of my stay. Nodding and smiling, I inhaled the familiar perfume of the house: a blend of amber, wood, butter, Shalimar perfume, and lingering oil from my grandpa's abandoned man cave downstairs.

As my nose adjusted to my surroundings and I listened to her chatter, I realized our perspectives of this new arrangement were markedly different. She felt she was taking care of me and that my safe guardianship required I keep runs within a four block radius. An impromptu call from my mom saved the day as she proclaimed, "Rach must be allowed to run free, Mom!" After this intervention, we settled into an easy rhythm, with me taking care of her and her taking care of me. Together we frosted her famous chocolate cake, picked strawberry rhubarb for tapioca pudding, and pulled the rickety blackberry ladder of death out of retirement so she could demonstrate (with monstrously large shears in hand) how to properly prune bushes. I prayed she would not topple from the top and die on my watch.

After lacing up in the mornings as my gram stared out a front window at small birds landing on an oak tree, my legs followed a familiar running route, through pretty parks and down a notoriously steep hill, until an endless ocean filled up the sky. Matching deep breaths with long strides as I raced alongside the boardwalk, the scent of rusted train-tracks and salty air stirred up vivid memories: brave cousins dancing into icy waves, thick ribbons of seaweed squishing between my toes, and my beautiful mother noshing on vinegar fries as I slurped down a DQ Mister Misty. Far exceeding my Griffith Park expectations, here on the Vancouver coast, without a man, career, or possessions, I felt grounded, centered, and safe. I might be searching for my place in the world, but I was not rootless.

As the days passed and I split my time between beach runs and pulling stubborn weeds, thin white tanks revealed my petite frame was shrinking. I wasn't shocked. A few months before, I'd noticed a slight gap between my legs; a beyond thrilling realization.

It's true then! I'm not so very different from other girls; I can lose weight! I'm in control and my body is responding. The winds of change are blowing!

The winds continued to blow as my abs became inverted. Although Zone Bars and Diet Coke were absent at my gram's house, a diet of small bran muffins, chicken breasts, and grilled vegetables dipped my weight lower, and then a bit lower still. Stepping onto my gram's green peppermint scale each morning, triumphant tears rolled down my face as I watched the needle drop; I was finally achieving a lightness of being! Fortunately for my shrinking stomach, I shared my gram's fondness for silky slices of her chocolate cake. In the evenings, we'd watched Guy Fieri taste-test cheesesteak empanadas and six-inch sandwiches on "Diners, Drive-Ins and Dives" as we dropped our forks into chocolatey bliss. Compared to the gluttony on the screen, I felt like a model of self-restraint as I scraped the last vestiges of frosting off my plate. My happiness was complete—nothing compared to enjoying slivers of cake as a skinny woman in complete control of her body!

This misplaced pride was checked one morning as I waited for the shower water to run hot. I'd stared at my nakedness ten years before in a similar morning light, but now my reflection was vastly different. Then my stomach resembled a plump powdered donut, my thighs thick trunks, and my butt a soft protrusion. Now exposed ribs stole the show from washboard abs, an extenuated clavicle, small round breasts, and a narrow face. Although relieved by the reduction of thigh and butt volume, I was horrified by this transformation. I was not a sexy Alessandra Ambrosio with high cheekbones and lean legs that go on for days. I was a velociraptor with hungry eyes on the hunt. Conflicting feelings permeated my insides as I polished my outsides with pungent grapefruit wash. I wanted to rejoice in my success—I was unquestionably skinny!—but my spirit was shaking with fear. Stepping forward from the recesses of my manipulated mind, my true self proclaimed my worth.

You deserve a healthy glow and full cheeks that radiate mirth! You deserve to feel strong and well, satiated and whole. You deserve to live!

A recognition of this truth, however, was overpowered by bitter tears that washed down the drain alongside tart suds. I'd fought tooth and nail for thinness; where was my supermodel body? What man would ever want to seduce, much less love me? No matter how intensive my commitment to thinness, I would never obtain the dimensions I craved; I could never be perfect. Perhaps I was destined to be a weak failure, unworthy of love. After slowly toweling off in soft cotton, I headed for the deck to find comfort in the arms of a woman far stronger than I imagined I would ever be.

SELF-LOVE GEM: CHOOSE ROLE MODELS OVER SUPERMODELS

A supermodel is not inherently admirable. Instead of imitating skin-deep beauty, seek role models who will inspire you to greatness. Which of your friends, public figures, or social media influencers are worth emulating? I'm drawn to people who treat others with kindness, beautify their spaces, and reach out to others with a generous heart. One woman I admire is a Peet's Coffee manager who demonstrates patience with her employees and greets every customer with a genuine smile. Another is a teacher who showers her Sociology students and sons with love while reserving time to connect with her friends. As I channel their strength while navigating the twists and turns of life, I look for ways to follow their leads and pay their goodness forward.

My family arrived at my gram's house a few days later for a brief visit that doubled as an intervention. Without mincing words, Brandon declared I looked scary thin and led me to the fridge to help him eat cake. Surrounded by the same loving support I'd experienced two years before, I increased my intake and watched as a healthy glow reappeared on my face. Although I wished to banish the gaunt velociraptor in the mirror, the strain of swallowing extra mouthfuls and experiencing fullness was excruciating. After years of herculean efforts to restrict, purposefully gaining weight ignited violent emotions. Was I eating too much and spiraling out of control? Was I on the fast-track to eating cheesesteak empanadas for breakfast? Anxious and confused, once my family disappeared and my gram and I settled back into our routine, I welcomed Mal's revised perspective on how to proceed.

A supermodel body is beyond my reach, but I can still demonstrate self-control by becoming "perfectly thin". There's a sweet-spot; a precise weight where I can remain a skinny blonde without looking like a sickly anorexic.

Zealously monitoring my body over the subsequent days, I hit this imaginary point one morning after a glorious coastal run. Happily sweating in black leggings and a grey sports bra, I stepped onto the peppermint scale to note what perfection looks like in black and white. It would be challenging to keep on the nose of this digit. One false move on my caloric tightrope —a turkey dinner or an ice cream sundae perhaps—would put everything at risk. If I could hold steady, however, I would radiate self-mastery, peace, and happiness as a Vancouver Sylvia deserving of praise and love.

12

THE SKINNY ON LOVESICK MONEYPENNY

VANCOUVER, CANADA: AGE 25

I rolled on lipstick, hiked up black stockings, and headed for the kitchenette. Never quite serrated enough, I twisted a stubborn english muffin apart and popped both sides into the toaster. As I reached for the peanut butter, my mind flitted between reviewing yesterday's food choices and mooning over James. While last night's grilled turkey sandwich elicited feelings of disappointment, my office crush triggered a fluttering of butterflies in my hollow insides. Beating wings mixed with growls as I smelled the salty sweetness of peanut butter. Using my best Skippy Mom hand motion, I filled toasted muffin craters with molten nut butter in back and forth movements. The aroma was intoxicating and I longed to pick up one piping hot side to take a bite. But this morning I would make myself proud; I would like myself more than yesterday. Carefully inserting my sticky lunch into a waiting Ziploc, I recommitted to having a good day (meaning a good food day) and stepped from my dark basement apartment into a brisk winter wind.

Traveling above the urban buzz by Skytrain (an electric

transit system running on elevated tracks), it's easy to believe you're arriving into Disney's Zootopia, Cloud City, or another futuristic society. A modern skyline flush with majestic glass buildings first catches your eye, but it's the beaches, parks, and harbors that quicken tourists' hearts as they speed into the bustling city center. It's debatable what's more inspiring: a frigid ocean swim on the westside or watching seaplanes land into Coal Harbour with a satisfying "whoosh!". Evoking Jon Krakauer's *Into the Wild,* Jack London's *White Fang,* and other northern adventure books, the whooshing of seaplanes can easily spark spontaneous excursions to one of Vancouver's nearby mountains. Traveling into the clouds by chairlift or climbing through northwestern trails is an enchanting way to recharge your soul while reigniting a belief that the universe is always on your side.

There was no time this morning for heavenly climbs. Stepping onto the jammed-packed train with my peanut butter muffin safely stored, my thoughts oscillated between James, my evening running route, and my gram. I wished my gram was up for a day trip into the city; she would have loved watching the seaplanes alight while tucking into a buttery lobster roll on a harbor patio. A month before, I'd kissed her cheek and promised to visit often as I packed my suitcase and caught the bus into the city. Leaving was unsettling; I worried she was lonely and felt leaving was an unkind decision. As the Skytrain arrived at Waterfront Station, I became mindful and squeezed through commuters to rush into the Tim Hortons donut stop located in the lobby of my office building. Soon I was ordering my usual while gaping at frosted donuts seductively entreating customers to be plucked out from their glass prison. "Good morning! I'd like two plain biscuits please! No, I don't want anything inside; just the biscuits. No, no butter either! Just those two biscuits right there, please. Yes, no drink; just two biscuits!"

After the Timmies worker and I got one another, I dropped a small takeaway bag into my purse and rode up the elevator. Once again, the means justified the ends; living in Vancouver was worth another round of managing Outlook calendars, arranging domestic travel, and ensuring an office was stocked with paperclips and tissue boxes. As a welcome change, however, this office was replete with kind humans and after readjusting my tights as I fetched our newspapers each morning, I'd assume my receptionist role at the front with pleasure and await James' entrance. The office's energy swelled when James arrived. Flush-faced after a brisk walk from his bachelor pad, he'd drop earbuds into his backpack as he recalled his marvelous last evening. As a Vancouver dandy, his evenings were always marvelous, and I listened with rapt attention as his Moneypenny until he disappeared into his office for the day.

Like many women, I could fill a small theater with unrequited loves. James' exceptional status in my little black book of crushes was his impact on my mental health. As evidenced from my morning rituals, hitting a sweet spot on a peppermint scale was not the end of my troubles! It was, in fact, far more difficult to maintain a precise digit on the scale than attempting to lose weight. Without any wiggle room, I was a slave to Mal's incessant commands and reminders.

Don't eat that! You'll get fat again! Wait, eat a bite of that, but, wait—no, that was too big of a bite! Why would you shove into your pie hole such a large forkful right then?

This mental minefield dissolved in James' company. My constant reel of nonsense—doubts, insecurities, food rumination—halted, and I became totally present. Momentarily released from Mal's clutches, I radiated my true self to become someone who, like James, manifests joy from the inside out.

There were a few glorious occasions I soared on hopeful wings I might become James' girl and thereby permanently free myself from mental torment. There was an invite to a buzzy Vancouver swing dancing night, which resulted in four minutes of twirling in James' arms before other women whisked him away for the night. There was a team hike up the Grouse Grind (Vancouver's notorious Stairmaster climb), which involved a top-down drive in James' car up a winding path I wished would continue forever. Most memorably, however, there was the office holiday party at a luxurious, rustic lodge in the woods where I dared to wish mistletoe magic might happen.

~

It was tipping down rain when I stepped out of a black taxi, but I was too nervous to care. A few weeks before, James had suggested I showcase my piano skills as part of the evening's entertainment to our party planner. After weeks of slipping into churches to memorize a piece as romantic and technically challenging as possible, Debussy's *Deux Arabesques* was stowed at the forefront of my mind. Taking off my wet coat and scarf, I mingled with my coworkers while nervously dipping crackers into baked brie blended with cranberry sauce. Across the way I spotted James looking fly in a fitted sports coat over a crisp white shirt. He caught my look, smiled broadly, and continued talking to a circle of enthralled listeners. Sick with adrenaline, I stuffed another festive cracker into my mouth and attempted to look as festively chill as possible. After what seemed like an eternity, our boss clinked his glass. "We are in for a treat tonight," he announced to an audience quietly sipping eggnog and wine. "Some of you are aware our Rachel is a classical pianist. She's agreed to play us something tonight, which I'm sure will be wonderful!"

I anxiously stepped towards the Grand piano in the center of the room, cracking a few cold knuckles before giving my fingers the signal to dance. The first forty seconds passed in a dreamlike haze as I skillfully ran complex trills and crescendoed at peak moments for dramatic effect. Once my fingers reached the second section of the piece, however, my mind went blank. I could not recall a single note. Staring down helplessly for inspiration, the black and white keys offered no assistance. I attempted to start again from the top, but it was useless; my memory required a complete reinstall.

"I'm so sorry!" I cried aloud, feeling my cheeks burn the shade of bright baubles on a nearby Christmas tree. Of course, this catastrophic embarrassment was handled beautifully by the crowd who clapped en masse.

"We love you Rachel—you needn't worry one bit," they merrily responded.

As I slinked away from the keys, I was offered encouraging smiles, cake, and glasses of holiday cheer. I didn't truly accept their compassion as I drowned my shame in a slice of spice cake. My life was over. I would quit the next morning—a lot more cake of the chocolate variety lay ahead in my future! Just then, however, as I finished a crumbly bite, James appeared. Bringing me in close with a comforting gesture, I caught a faint smell of oranges, bourbon, and amber. "That first part was wonderful Rach; really, it was. You've impressed us all; well done!" Empty plates with half-eaten cake slices soon piled up on tables and, before too long, coats and scarves were zipped and layered as drowsy revelers waited for their taxis to arrive. As I joined the party on a covered step and watched heavy rain beat down, James caught my arm from behind. "Merry Christmas Rachel," he whispered, while moving in for a close embrace. His flushed eggnogg'd cheek and strong arms relinquished my residual embarrassment; I lingered against him for an instant, soaking in powerful emotions of warmth and love.

Is it greedy to want to feel this good?—I wondered as I slid into the back seat of a taxi.

Do I deserve to feel this happy after this taxi turns back into a pumpkin? Can I be good enough in the arms of a man? Will anyone love me if I expose myself as an anorexic woman?

I was unaware self-hatred, not romance, was keeping joy at a distance. Rather than looking outwards, I needed to direct loving vibes inwards; to treat myself with the same kindness I bestowed on others. This isn't to disqualify my affection for James. My silent love was a sliver of heaven during a trying time inside my disorder. I do wish, however, I had believed James was just as lucky to feel the warmth of my heart that night as I was to feel his cheek against mine.

~

As jarring as it seems, it was August and I was moving again. This move didn't come out of the blue! As I departed LA the previous summer, Shawn, in his usual insightful advisor role, had suggested I hedge my bets by applying to UK teaching programs. Shocked by an acceptance to Cambridge's teacher's college that spring, I concluded the university was simply interested in my international tuition fees. Still, on the heels of my Christmas performance, I was proud to announce to my office that I was more than a receptionist with a crap memory and commenced packing my suitcase for another adventure across the pond. James waltzed up to reception one afternoon as I munched on one of my last Vancouver peanut butter muffins. "Rach! You're leaving! Let's catch dinner before you disappear forever!" I was furious. After months of waiting, he was asking me out now? As with my school acceptance, I swiftly manipulated his invitation into something sour.

He's asking me now because there will be no complications, just a one-off date. He doesn't like me; he's just being nice.

Regardless, I spent the next seventy-two hours searching for the perfect outfit and thanked my lucky stars I could squeeze into a flowered crop-top that perfectly coordinated with a pretty pink clutch. Holding tightly onto my new fashion accessory as we met on the beach, the butterflies in my cage flitted about mercilessly. They continued to bounce about for the rest of the night as we dined on grilled chicken, olives, and pita, and then walked along the sand. I might have floated to England when he kissed me goodnight in beachy moonlight. He might not want to date me, but at least I was kissable! Convinced this all meant *something*, I recalled this moment throughout the next year when I felt lonely, pathetic, or unwanted. If even for just one night, I was thin enough, cute enough, fun enough, and altogether good enough, just as I am.

SELF-LOVE GEM: BELIEVE THE GOOD

Compliments are opportunities to honor our self-worth. After years of adhering to a false belief that I am not good enough, I found it impossible to accept any applause, no matter how small. Rather, I downgraded compliments (she's just being nice), or worse, turned praise into something negative (she likes my makeup because my outfit looks ridiculous). How often do you pay insincere compliments? Probably not very often! Shouldn't you, then, believe the good aimed in your direction? And why not supplement the kindness you receive by feeding your soul with positive affirmations? Remind yourself of your value, consider what small features you love about yourself, and reaffirm—out loud if necessary— that you are a valuable person who deserves kindness and respect! By bolstering your self-worth on a regular basis, you'll be prepared to face the challenges ahead and feel inspired to pay compliments forward.

SECTION IV: RIGID TIMES WITH LOW LOWS & HIGH HIGHS

13

RUNNING ON A WORKAHOLIC BUZZ

CAMBRIDGE, ENGLAND: AGE 26

The University of Cambridge is seriously pretty and unequivocally vintage. Still radiating old world charm today, Zara and Jo Malone are housed in elegant stone structures while meadows grow wild alongside a winding river without fearing Walmart or modern apartments will threaten their survival. Behind its charming facade, however, the university harbors a torrent of anxiety, which I effortlessly assumed on my first day as I took a seat at the Faculty of Education. Adjusting the fitted beige jacket I'd selected that morning, I attempted to radiate California cool as a classroom of strangers and I waited for our instructor to appear. When she did appear, bearing armfuls of crafty materials and workbooks, Cara blew us away with her over-the-top exuberance. A long bob bouncing playfully around her face, she sectioned us into groups to scribble down everything we knew about British History onto broad sheets of butcher paper. Cara was a superhuman with enough publications, degrees, prominent positions, breakups and breakdowns to qualify as an academic goddess. More importantly, her passion for history and education was genuine and infectious; within days I was under her spell and anxious to win her approval.

Consequently, I was elated to be assigned to Mary, one of Cara's previous top students, as my practical experience mentor. The Head of History at a nearby school, Mary was a perfectionist who seamlessly juggled teaching with writing quotable articles in educational magazines. Although she wasn't particularly stylish, her fitted dark outfits were smartly pulled together with cable knits I suspected she designed in a very tidy home decorated with seasonal florals and a collection of mismatched coffee cups. Under her watchful brown eyes, I taught dozens of lessons to teenage students who were delighted by my American accent. Mary kept her cards close while observing my lessons from the back of her classroom. Although I routinely burnt my oil past midnight to design exceptional lessons, I was certain she lamented to her husband each night, "She's overwhelmingly energetic, but my word she's an idiot!" My world imploded the moment she raised an eyebrow from the back as I explained a concept or answered a student's question. Sweaty and panicked, I'd immediately switch gears, keen to divert her attention back on her students.

Walking briskly to catch my ride back to Cambridge one afternoon, I peeked my head into Mary's classroom to wish her goodnight. She might believe I'm a silly American, but she must like me; on this point I was firm! Sipping coffee while enjoying a piece of sticky toffee cake, Mary waved me inside with a free hand. As I approached her desk, I kissed my ride home goodbye and enviously eyeballed her cake. She looked at me with a twinkle in her eye. Then her lips curled into a faint smile. I assumed cake was behind this merriment as she carefully slid another forkful into her mouth. She paused to swallow before speaking. "Your Revolutionary War lesson was lovely Rachel; the students enjoyed it very much. What a sweet way to introduce Historical Significance. How about we hash out the concept more right now; I can give you a lift home if you'd like?"

Mary's proposition superseded any happiness over this unexpected praise. My heart fell like heavy cream into her coffee cup as I envisioned all the work still waiting for me back home. Far more horrifying, however, was the postponement of tonight's dinner. Restricting was reaching lofty heights in Cambridge. Pushed to my emotional brink, I didn't realize many of my peers weren't completing Cara's course readings or marking every student's work with careful precision. I was the naïve woman on that train, steaming towards exhaustion in the name of gold stars and approval. Furthermore, I'd unwittingly gained weight since arriving in England due to late night Cadbury chocolate treats and the ever present cookie tin in school lounges. Determined to feel in control and to return to a lightness of being, I denied my body as best I could during the day. This worked well in theory since, apart from a school shop selling sandwiches and cakes (hence Mary's sticky toffee number), the only viable food option was the cafeteria, which I avoided at all costs. And yet, although I was adept at riding out hunger pangs and resisting a student's Funfetti birthday cupcakes, I was not a robot. By 6:00 p.m., I was on edge and fixated on an impending release from starvation.

Consequently, Mary's proposal hit my brain like a category four hurricane. A people pleasing instinct overpowering my base needs, I felt powerless to resist. Besides, how could I speak my shameful truth?

I'm a failing anorexic who might not look super-skinny but who is famished and finding it impossible to concentrate. I need to go home immediately!

Without an escape route, I popped the top off a squeaky black marker and, fuming with resentment and defeat, joined

Mary at the board to draw phrases, concentric circles, and linking arrows across a large white surface for the next two hours. Every now and again, I glanced over to see Mary scribbling away with purposeful intent. I wanted to be on her level, considering the subtle differences of "significance" and "meaning" while jotting down criteria for what makes an event significant. Try as I might, however, I could not truly engage; I was too weak, too shaky, and too preoccupied with the toffee cake crumbs on Mary's plate to care. Fortunately, at the very moment I feared I might faint and smear board marker with my cheek while falling, Mary squeezed the top back onto a marker. Standing back, she assessed our effort with meticulous scrutiny. "Let's call this done, shall we?" she beamed a moment later. "I can't wait to tell Cara about our creative session; what a productive activity!"

After capturing pictures of the board, Mary took me home in her grey Honda Fit. As we zoomed around corners, I thought how delightful this experience might have been under different circumstances. With a handful of baby carrots and a tablespoon of nut butter moving through my system, I could have approached the board with confidence. There were, however, no tide me over carrots in my ED world. Snacks were dangerous! What if I ate eight baby carrots and then realized I should have only eaten four? What if I could not stop spooning out nut butter? Dinner could be spoiled; the whole night could be spoiled! Exhausted, I smiled at Mary as she shifted up a gear while chatting about her American husband learning to drive in the UK. Thankfully she was leading the conversation so I could think properly and reassure my stomach that food was on the way.

Gently sighing with relief as the Cambridge sign came into view, I realized this was our first connection. I'd wondered for weeks if there was a personality hiding out in Mary's cable knit sweaters. I still couldn't imagine her belting out Whitney Houston at Karaoke, but just like me, she possessed a deep and divine soul that craved connection and acceptance. Today she'd been inspired to collaborate with another history nerd as a mentor and also as a friend. I had dreamt of situations like this while racing to Starbucks and copying stacks of paperwork for bosses. Now that my moment had arrived, however, I'd been too hangry to enjoy it. Stepping out of Mary's Honda, I waved goodbye and ran inside to feed a hollow belly.

By Christmas, I was shattered from work but wild about Cambridge. Angelic choral concerts, clusters of meadow cows flapping their ears in the wind, and the chocolate shop passing out milky samples I'd drop into a cold pocket for later: small pleasures softened my pain and tied my heart to the town. Feelings of achievement transcended any regrets over leaving Vancouver as I flew home for Christmas that year. In fact, my happiness felt all the more acute because of my struggles. After months of twenty-hour work days, I was entitled to a good rest! I deserved to flip through a glossy magazine while sipping on cranberry juice and staring at puffy clouds outside my British Airways window. I could justify a lazy repose to connect with family, friends, and holiday cinnamon rolls. I would inevitably regret the rolls, but there was no doubt I deserved to savor the tastes of cinnamon, nutmeg, and sweetly salted butter.

~

Buoyed up with festive cheer, I sprinted into a new year to battle my way through a brutal winter and a stormy spring of unremitting work. Dashing into the meadows at dawn and dancing on sticky floors at night provided temporary relief from stress, but these expressions of self-care were too rare to right my boat. An emancipated love junkie would have shifted the balance to honor her needs and limitations. She would have worked hard, of course, but with the belief that not every lesson needs to be perfect and that skipping a reading for the sake of sleep is sometimes the right choice. Instead, determined to be perfect and afraid of failure, I worked myself to exhaustion until I slipped on a lace dress for graduation day. Staring at my reflection in a full-length mirror, euphoric feelings once more validated a masochistic "no pain, no gain" approach to life. Although I abhorred anorexia's impact on my life, I was relieved my dress effortlessly draped over my body without encountering any cumbersome folds or rolls. I wasn't at my Vancouver ideal digit, but I had halted the tide of fatness. Paired with nods and smiles of approval from Cara and Mary as I walked across a graduation stage, my lace buttons burst with pride. Today I was exuding my worthiness! Today I was good enough! Determined to continue along this trajectory—to fit into lace dresses and collect the hardest to reach gold stars—I ecstatically accepted an offer to teach History and Politics at Hills Road Sixth Form, a high achieving school in the heart of Cambridge.

SELF-LOVE GEM: DESIGN A BALANCED REALITY

Many humans struggle with procrastination. If, however, you're a high-functioning perfectionist, you may feel compelled to rise and shine at 7:00 a.m. on Sundays to smooth fresh sheets onto beds or to lace up your sneakers for a morning run. Being a go-getter is great, except when drive becomes a roadblock on the highway to happiness. There's no lasting pleasure in testing your limits in the name of "productivity" or "achievement". Balance is essential in creating a sustainable and healthy lifestyle. Setting aside time for reflection and relaxation is far from lazy! Rather, our bodies and brains need chill time to help us live in a smarter and more refined way. It is when we slacken our pace and smell the proverbial roses that we are best equipped to exude the most vibrant versions of ourselves.

14

BITTERSWEET EXHAUSTION

CAMBRIDGE, ENGLAND: AGE 27

For once in my life a new chapter surpassed my lofty expectations. Within the first week of teaching, I was head over knee-high boots in love with my students, colleagues, and roommates, not to mention my cinematic Jane Austen-esque bicycle commute across town. This isn't to say I was winning at life. Teaching British and American Politics without a clue who is in which cabinet is sticky, as is creating Modern History lessons without knowing Lenin wasn't a member of the Beatles. The course titles, however, sounded sexy to a history nerd and the harder the better, right? Consequently, throwing caution into the River Cam, I charged ahead into two more years of high-highs and low-lows.

The lows were annoyingly low. Twenty-hour work days and a merciless ED stripped away at my well-being. Attempting to deliver faultless lessons required me to be the first woman on campus each day and to avoid "wastes of time" like doctor appointments, lunch, and the loo to devote every second to work. After supporting my brain with Diet Coke, white rolls, bananas, and nuts over thirteen hours, a stop at the gym to burn non-existent calories was my guilty pleasure before arriving home to feed my wilting body on bread, cheese, tomatoes, and avocado. Hiking upstairs to bed, I'd seek serenity in the luxurious white sheets I'd splurged on as I drifted into teaching dreams. Unfortunately, no matter how hard I worked from sunrise to sunset, one victory was never enough. My principal's praise on Friday was splendid, but what about the following Monday? Would I fail on Monday? If I was an ace teacher one week, was I falling short in other ways? Was I sneaking too many cookies from the staff tin on breaks? Was I not enthusiastic enough (as a young American teacher *should* be!) at every single parent-teacher conference? Did I forget that mousy girl's name or confuse Jack's report with Jake's?

Weekends offered a respite; a diet version of my intensive lifestyle. After a liberating ten-mile run to revive my spirits, I'd wash my luxe sheets, mark hundreds of essays, and then cycle into town to continue my search for the perfectly curated minimalist wardrobe. This self-sabotaging venture was particularly silly, since I demanded each piece flawlessly complement my aesthetic, be precisely tailored to my frame, align with the other pieces in my closet, and cost exactly what I wished to pay, which wasn't much. Bound to fail, I never located items fast enough, hated on my body in badly lit dressing rooms, and, after hours of wandering in circles with decision paralysis, purchased something I would inevitably regret and return for store credit the following weekend. Manically racing about on errands and squeezing in time to shave my legs and call home, I could not be calm. Attempts to attend church as a spiritual boost were futile. Running low on faith and zeal, I found sitting through a multi-hour service hard work. There was little free time in my life and, as I watched the minutes ticked by, I longed to feel the wind on my face as I ran through the wild meadows. Instead of absorbing any gems I heard from my pew,

I latched onto anxiety-inducing admonitions to become more perfect, and, with guilt and detachment outstripping my devotion, I turned to friends and nature to chill out my manic mind and fatigued body.

Sometimes a chill pill came in the form of a green chicken curry a roommate passed into my cold hands when I arrived home late. Other times a hike through a winding trail in England's Peak District slowed my wheels. On the flip-side of calm, throwing holiday parties became my hands-down favorite distraction. Running a piñata out a window to wack from the street below on Cinco de Mayo was surprisingly satisfying, as was baking a line-up of pumpkin pies well into the wee morning hours to celebrate American Thanksgiving. Whether demonstrating my hostess with the mostess ambitions or escaping somewhere sunny for a girls' holiday, bonding, present experiences in good company provided a necessary break from my crazy. On rare occasions, good company included romantic moments, like the July morning I nibbled on canelé pastries with a stranger on a French hillside. Drowsy after our mutual friend's wedding party, I suddenly only knew the taste of vanilla, a clear blue sky, and simple, flirtatious conversation. We rendezvoused a few more times in London and Cambridge over the summer, indulging ourselves in the same peaceful happiness and connection we'd enjoyed on the hillside, until I left England and our canelé magic drifted into the recesses of my memory.

SELF-LOVE GEM: NURTURE POSITIVE RELATIONSHIPS

Relationships are an invaluable feature of life. Happily, we are designed to feel our best when we reach out and link with others! Although I craved friendships and affection in my twenties, I felt guilty when I took a girls' holiday or supported someone through a break-up; I worried I should be working on something more "important". As an emancipated love junkie, I now realize enjoying cupcakes with a friend or bringing soup to a sick neighbor are meaningful opportunities to feel the love that comes from bonding with others. Consider what positive relationships you'd like to create or nurture, not because you should but because of the happiness you can give and the good vibes you can receive. And then, reach out!

I bit into a hard cookie as I typed my final student reports one rainy June afternoon. My visa was expiring and, as Hills Road College and England politely opened the back door, I once more wondered, *Where do I go from here?* I'd assumed the morning I took a seat in Cara's classroom three years before that I'd be loved-up with a Brit by this time, or signing a fall contract to work in an American school. Frankly, however, the idea of learning a new curriculum and marking thousands of new students' essays was daunting at best. Shattered after years of hyper-producing, I was realizing my limitations and craving a work/life balance. Although I'd be lost without purpose, I would never be a Cara or a Mary! I refused to devote my entire life to others as a model teacher, extracurricular hero, or departmental head fighting fires and managing personalities—and I was increasingly okay with this fact. At the present, my ambitions centered around dating eligible guys, baking cookies, and waking up well rested to gaze at ocean waves crashing onto a shoreline.

Consequently, an unexpected call that afternoon from sunny California was perfectly timed. My brothers were running a boutique production company in the Hollywood Hills, and with pre-production underway Shawn and Brandon were hopeful I'd join their team as a scriptwriter.

"Are you interested, Rach? Shawn and I know you'll be perfect for the job and, well, you should be here with us! I don't want you to miss out on this adventure!"

I didn't need time to consider. This was a one-way ticket to purpose, sunshine, and a low-stress, easy happiness; I'd be insane not to accept.

"You know I'm in; don't have too much fun until I get there!"

Tacos, guacamole, sunshine, and swaying palms filled the spaces of my mind as I settled my luggage onto a train heading towards Heathrow Airport. As the train steamed out of the station, my heart heaved with bittersweet exhaustion. I could hardly wait to run into the Pacific and bite into a hotdog at a baseball stadium heaving with ardent Dodgers' fans. And yet, I was gutted to leave a place I adored that was filled with beautiful memories, to include escapades with girlfriends who loved me in spite of my flaws. Yes, I mused as the outskirts of town disappeared from view, the lows were so low, but the highs were so wonderfully high I had almost touched the clouds.

15

HELLO WORLD, I AM WONDER WOMAN

LOS ANGELES, CALIFORNIA: AGE 29

S hawn rolled up to the Delta Airlines curb in a retro BMW, looking LA cool in Ray-Bans, black jeans, and a fitted black t-shirt. After dumping my battered luggage into the trunk, we sped north on the 405 highway past Westwood and Century City before turning northwards. Rising above the heat and grit of the Sunset Strip, the Hollywood Hills provides glamorous seclusion as well as stunning views of the city. Turning sharply and accelerating around corners, we climbed upwards past chrome driveways, formidable yet nondescript entrances, manicured palm trees, and pedigreed pups until we reached the top of Blue Jay Way. There, towering above the city below, stood an imposing white mansion my brothers were renting as a production studio/crew accommodation. Drowsily stretching in the sunshine as Shawn grabbed my bags, I wondered what I could expect from the next six months at this surreal palace. Would I be happy here? A moment later I was standing inside a large foyer flooded with sunlight as strangers abandoned their MacBooks to meet the new screenwriter. Glazed over after thirty hours of travel, I shook hands as quickly as possible and, like Snow White, stumbled upstairs to find a soft spot to sleep.

~

I bolted upright at 5:45 a.m., my hair a wreck and my heart beating quickly.

What have I done?

Scriptwriting in Los Angeles sounds crazy, sexy, cool when you're thousands of miles away in a soggy British rain. But now, waking up in a strange Hollywood mansion, my reality seemed ludicrous.

I don't belong here! What have I done?—I repeated to myself.

I fumbled in the darkness for running shoes and shorts and then scampered downstairs. The traffic had yet to appear on the streets as I descended down our impossibly steep street to the base of Sunset Boulevard and headed southwards. A late summer breeze whisked soft citrus, jasmine, and dewy notes into my nose and, as I stretched out my legs and inhaled deeply, I calmly considered my situation. Could I actually write a script? Apart from essays, short stories, and an occasional blog post, my portfolio was slim. And yet, I'd been invited to write; this was no handout and I was not a charity case. I might come at a bargain basement sibling price, but my brothers were confident I'd produce something good—or at least good enough.

Why can't I write a script? I've taught politics at a British school without realizing Margaret Thatcher was kind of a big deal. I've recorded two albums with my brother without an agent or studio. I've survived a Chinese endoscopy without anesthetic! Besides, my brothers are counting on me.

"Of course I can do it!" I said aloud to the universe, which at that instant appeared in the form of a café worker setting out chairs for sidewalk diners.

～

I arrived back at the top of the Blue Jay Way feeling rapturously fatigued. Stretching my arms upwards towards the sky, I jubilantly estimated I'd completed a half marathon before 8:oo a.m.

Today I am Wonder Woman, with enough brains and brawn to save the universe!

A growling belly interrupted this exhilaration with a message that something tasty was long overdue.

Yes, yes! It's time for breakfast. But first, a cold dip to mark this new era of my life!

Slipping back into the darkness, I snuck upstairs to locate a bikini and a towel, and then headed back outside to step onto the pool deck. My core was still hot and my forehead releasing beads of sweat as I surveyed the skyscape. A thousand feet up from Sunset Boulevard, Los Angeles seemed so quiet and peaceful. Was it really four years since I'd lived here before? Had I changed for the better or was I now just a bit older with more addresses under my extra-small belt? Vowing to make this year a remarkable one, I cannonballed into placid water, shimmering in the sunlight. Like biting into a Popsicle on a sweltering August day, an intense sensation instantly chilled my steamy body. Flailing my arms and legs about in aqua marine surroundings, I welcomed the heady combo of exhaustion and hunger while blowing cold water through my nose and swaying liberated hair in all directions. Radiating strength and happiness, I pulled myself out of the water, grabbed my towel, and dashed inside to top off my solitude with a hot shower.

As I readjusted white cotton beneath my underarm and

ambled towards the stairs, a figure jolted my body to full attention. I apprehensively leapt backwards, my body on flight alert. Who was there? Was this a masked intruder? My eyes adjusting to the light, I realized all was well. This was not a thief but a production crew member meandering towards the kitchen. He was dark complexioned and slim, dressed in a well-loved yellow Elvis t-shirt and plaid shorts. Donning an array of bracelets and necklaces, he appeared as a merry sailor who'd just anchored after exotic escapades on distant islands. Equally surprised to find a girl dripping pool water all over the floor (not exactly the James Bond/Honey Ryder moment I might have wished), he smiled broadly and held out a firm right hand. "Good morning! I'm Cody, the new line producer; I flew in from Panama last night. I'm sorry if I frightened you. I didn't think anyone else was up!" I couldn't help noticing his other hand was clasping *Line Producing for Dummies*. While this didn't inspire confidence in his skills, who was I to judge? Two hours before I'd been a hopeless, inexperienced writer without a drop of faith in myself. Besides, his manner was confident and friendly. Yes, I liked this guy; he could continue towards the kitchen with my blessing. Bounding up the stairs with a smile, I instinctively felt Cody and I would get to know each other very well.

~

An hour later, clean and refreshed, I walked back onto Sunset Boulevard and tucked into Café Primo with my head held high.

Hello world, I am Wonder Woman and I deserve to be here, just like everyone else! Make way for the superhero scriptwriter!

Sterile slab high top seats, tall white ceilings with exposed beams, and a smoothie menu written in black script presented an attractive, clean atmosphere. In this modern sanctuary I felt inspired to shine as a strong and confident California Sylvia. Here I would shed my Cadbury chocolate pounds to become a skinny (but not too skinny!) anorexic. Here I would launch my writing career by creating something marvelous. And here I would enjoy a scrumptious breakfast deserving of a Wonder Woman who ran thirteen miles before breakfast. But what to pick? An extensive medley of smells permeated the café: aromatic espresso filling tiny glasses, sweet waffles crisping on the press, and fresh kale, beets, and ginger whirling away in Vitamixes. Ordering a tall glass of iced water and the gooiest banana muffin I'd ever seen, I took a seat at a high top, clicked in my charger, and got to the business of writing—after enveloping my senses in molten banana love, that is.

The imagination is a wonderful place, immune to the trash-talk of an inner critic. Creating a character's backstory or devising a "meet cute" (like my recent bikini moment with Cody) became pure escapism; a chance to elude my ED while transforming raw energy into something beautiful. As banana bites fueled my belly and brain, busy fingers filled a white screen with text until Primo's lunch rush ignited a minor revolution in my belly. Coming up for air, I assessed the current landscape as my gut weighed in on my next move.

Yes, yes! The muffin was fine but what about now?—it seemed to inquire. *What else can keep me quiet for another eight hours?*

Tiptoeing across the narrow tightrope I'd balanced on for years, I ordered a Diet Coke and a pack of almonds, scarfing them down as quickly as possible.

There! Now time to refocus!

As I settled back into writing, however, I couldn't help noticing a number of super-fit women meeting up with friends or scrolling through their phones at nearby tables. Glistening with sweat from the posh gym next door, they'd come for goat cheese frittatas, roasted tomato quiches, and kale smoothies. This wasn't my first time checking out Sylvias who dine. Ever since spying a gorgeous Manhattanite twirling her pasta on a cold winter night, I'd witnessed vast amounts of food entering the dainty mouths of put-together women. On top of their pocketbooks and ritzy lifestyles, I'd believed their advanced bodies kept me out of their elitist club. Operating at peak performance (regardless of hormones or stress), I'd assumed their metabolisms sprinted like adorable field mice on platinum wheels while a pudgy hamster, without an ounce of stamina or spirit, operated my system. Now, however, after extensive work to fashion an idyllic body, the gulf between us didn't sit well.

Why can't I confidently enjoy a frittata? Why must I try so hard to feel comfortable in my skin? I don't want to starve anymore! I want to feel normal and enjoy life too!

But I couldn't enjoy life; not yet. Oozing chill happiness is impossible when an abusive voice is suffocating your soul. Thinking outside the ED box with an open mind is an equally laughable and frightening idea. I couldn't possibly maintain a slim figure if I ate real food during daylight hours! There's no way a salad filled with veg could supersede a "safe" muffin! Entrenched rules were in place to keep me binge-free and on track; was I really willing to risk experiencing immense fullness or spiraling out of control to step outside my boundaries? A cool breeze of change was softly blowing, but it would take years before I broke through my ED prison walls to pursue love. The thing is, anorexia is far more complicated than skinny jeans and frittatas! A polished Sylvian facade was desirable, but my true ambition was to rise above a hardwired belief that I am not good enough by proving myself worthy of praise and love in a myriad of ways. Eventually I would crush this limiting belief to become an emancipated love junkie, but for the time being, as I gazed at Primo's Sylvias and kissed my work/life balance dreams goodbye to meet others' needs, I recognized my perspective on life was warped and my trust in Mal misplaced. Thankfully, as a constant craving to design a kinder reality simmered, the Sylvian goddesses in my view began to lose their false brilliance and melted into gold puddles in the West Hollywood heat.

SELF-LOVE GEM: HONOR YOUR HUNGER

More than a decade after suspiciously staring at cafeteria cakes, I was exhausted from restricting but unwilling to expunge destructive habits. I wish I had realized at Primo that life is meant to be sweet and wonderful! Our bodies send us hunger cues out of care and protection, not as a way to torture us with grumbles and growls. You deserve to honor your cues and enjoy the fruits of proper nutrition, to include a strengthened body, a calm brain, and a happy heart. It might be challenging to bite into something satisfying at the moment, but remind yourself throughout each day that you deserve to eat well and often! Positive self-talk is a wonderful way to show yourself kindness as you step forward on a path towards enlightened Recovery.

16

CHASING SUNSETS

LOS ANGELES, CALIFORNIA: AGE 29

It was October and I was polishing off the final scenes of my draft at the top of Blue Jay Way. After weeks of ten-hour writing shifts at Primo, collaborating with my bikini "meet cute" was a breath of arctic fresh air. Not only was Cody chock-full of ideas on how to rectify plot gaps, but full of boyish charm he also became my go-to for a purple Sour Patch Kid or a hit of good ol' fashioned flirting. I was revising a scene on the deck one afternoon when Cody took me by the hand and whispered, "Wanna get out of here, Rach? Let's chase the sunset!" I grinned with excitement as we sped down the hill in pursuit of a waning sun on the horizon. Peeling down aptly named Sunset, we followed the twists and turns of the boulevard until we reached Santa Monica, just in the nick of time.

As the sun began its nightly performance, gracefully dropping like a silent pebble behind the ocean, I zipped up my jacket and intertwined my arms and fingers with Cody. The colors overhead shifted from light oranges and reds to dramatic ambers and maroons as we laughed and shared stories in the dusky light. I felt so alive; so peaceful and glowing. I hadn't pieced it together yet. It wasn't croissants or canelé pastries, James or Cody, or stunning sunrises or sunsets that elicited blissful emotions in my heart. Rather, like a cold wind sweeping through a forest, life's loveliest moments shook the stale and useless thoughts out of my mind. In this instance, enveloped in nature's beauty and love, I briefly experienced life as a love junkie—free to witness the world with clear eyes and a thankful heart. Anxious to tap into this goodness, I welcomed Cody's company into the holiday season, and, by our team's New Year's Eve pool party bash, we were crushing on each other hard as we planned voyages to far off places and steamed down Sunset to chase a resplendent sun.

SELF-LOVE GEM: BE PRESENT

When we live in the present and become immune to negative thoughts, it becomes easy to notice the gems on our path and to appreciate our relationships. Staying present in a world of distractions takes practice. Along with yoga and short meditations, mindfulness is an excellent way to focus our monkey brains. Give it a try! Maybe take two minutes today to stare at the clouds, marveling at the shapes you see and noticing the speed at which they drift across the sky. Or listen to a song you love and consider why you're drawn to the melody and the lyrics. Just taking two minutes to press pause on your thoughts will help you to reconnect with your true self while enjoying the pleasures of the here and now.

Between sunrises and sunsets, life became increasingly stressful. Onboarding a production crew while locking down a script, shooting locations, and a diva-free cast was expected chaos, but having our studio's investment funds trapped in India was not. As the viability of our operation became increasingly precarious, the mansion erupted with palpable hysteria. Delayed salaries brought out the worst in disgruntled staff members who transitioned from acquiring set props and securing filming permits to watching Fox's *How I Met Your Mother* reruns in hidden nooks. As petty dramas and power trips abounded à la MTV's *Real World* style, I wished the team would swallow a giant chill pill and exude SoCal cool.

Occasionally, a trip to Mel's Drive-In at the base of Sunset Boulevard mollified hotheads with hot eats and cool treats. On high caloric and confrontation alert, I watched as the crew clamoured to servers in white shirts and black ties—

"I'll take a patty melt with extra cheese, and twisty fries too!"

"A Melburger with onion rings for me!"

"An extra-thick banana milkshake here!"

Bent out of shape lips curved upwards as ginormous shakes topped with cherries appeared, served alongside steel mixing cups with extra swirled cream. You know, just in case a glass wasn't enough. Particularly horrifying was one meaty guy's order of not one, but two entrees for himself—apparently he and I dealt with stress in very different ways.

Long distance runs through Beverly Hills, cookie bakes, and Cody became my salvation during our final weeks at the mansion. As Cody enthusiastically recalled his sailing adventures around the Caribbean, I'd pop Snickerdoodles and Chocolate-Chip Cookies into the oven to soothe tempers while testing out riffs on recipes I'd toyed with since Cambridge. Consequently, when the shakes hit the fan and the production halted, I returned to the world below Sunset Boulevard with Cody, a pocketful of customized cookie notes, and a plan. Rash yet thrilling, Cody and I were moving to Charleston, South Carolina to start a very different kind of adventure together; a chill one centered around warm skies and pecan pies, coastal drives and easy-breezy, lovin' vibes. On the heels of Cambridge and Los Angeles, creating a simple southern life in the company of my guy shone like a beacon of happiness I couldn't wait to chase.

Moving to Charleston demanded I break my vault wide open. Cody already suspected something was up with my dietary habits; how could I move across the country with a man without first addressing the skinny rhino pirouetting in my kitchen? After days of delaying the inevitable, a spontaneous trip to the Olive Garden presented an ideal moment for a confessional. I was tucking into shrimp scampi as Cody launched into his perspective on Diet Coke. "Everyone knows regular is way tastier. Anyone ordering a plate of carbs and cream shouldn't care less if it's Diet!" My anxiety ticked upwards with each creamy bite of asparagus. Apart from the fact that I was currently drinking Diet, Cody was unwittingly attacking my way of life. Diet Coke was my rock; my safe harbor in a sea of creamy sauces, juicy burgers, and saucy shrimp! Its cola bubbles thrilled my neglected taste buds and kept my hunger at bay during the long, often torturous hours between meals. How dare he vilify Diet without any comprehension of what it meant to a girl like me!

I furiously pushed aside my plate, still half full of pasta but cleaned of veg and shrimp. "I need to explain something to you this instant!" I cried out. "Please don't interrupt; I'm far too nervous to make it through if you interrupt!" It took a whole thirty seconds to get the "A" word out of my lemon and garlicky mouth. I might as well have been confessing multiple previous marriages, hidden children, and sordid affairs. My body shook as the words pushed forward from my heart into my vocal cords. "I'm anorexic, Cody." There was a long pause before I continued. "I have been for years; it's a significant part of who I am. I thought you should know."

The tears came streaming down my cheeks as our server approached to gauge our interest in the Black Tie Mousse. Glancing at my face, he quickly retreated to the kitchen. Cody cradled my exposed hand between both of his. "Rach, thank you for telling me," he said softly, "but it's no big deal; we can handle this or anything else together." Relief washed over my body as I felt the strength of his hands. He truly cared and was willing to love and support me, regardless of my black spot. All was well. Such was my feeling as we skipped the mousse and asked for the check. As I replayed this scene over the next few days, however, I reconsidered my feelings.

Anorexia is the sorrow of my life! It ruins everything; it strips all my happiness! I hate it more than anything or anyone! Should I be furious at Cody for minimizing a decade of pain? Should I hate him for his ignorance of anorexia's horrors?

Then again, maybe it isn't a big deal; at least not anymore. Maybe now, in Cody's company, I can become an effortlessly skinny and happy woman, free of mental torment!

Brimming with optimism as I hugged Shawn and Brandon goodbye a few days later, I squeezed into a packed car heading eastwards. Rolling down the window and turning up Katy Perry's "Wide Awake" on the dial, I kissed old Rachel farewell to assume the guise of a happy and skinny southern blonde whose food issues were really no big deal.

SECTION V: REACHING MY MELTING POINT

17

PATISSERIE & POPSICLE DREAMS

CHARLESTON, SOUTH CAROLINA: AGE 30

Cody and I moved into a green apartment complex in Charleston's historic downtown. Teeming with stretches of white beaches, romantic historic homes, mazes of cobblestone streets, and roadside stands advertising salty boiled peanuts, South Carolina surpassed all my southern fantasies. Racing into the sweltering heat in shorts and shades, Cody and I explored every nook and cranny of our new world. After gleefully collecting history site brochures and peppering tour guides with questions, we'd return home to cold showers and hot scallops that sizzled in brown butter before plopping into bowls holding creamy pasta and seasoned spinach. Then, with bowls in hand and fresh cotton against clean skin, we'd cozy up in cushions to drift into food comas while watching slow-paced Civil War documentaries.

Cody was an unexpected ED safety net. Food rituals snapped back into place and the burden of food choices lifted as we whipped up delicious meals together. However, as I inevitably lamented downing too many scallops and lost it over midday gelato, Cody and I accepted my disorder was, in fact, a *very big deal.* Thankfully, morning runs and evening strolls along Charleston's harbor smoothed my rumpled spirits and tempered anorexic sorrows. Snuggling down in sweatshirts while intertwining chilly fingers together, we'd listen to a quartet playing on the balcony of a historic mansion before looping northwards where southern tunes drifted out of rooftop bars.

Across the street from our complex, a small patisserie added an additional luster to our world. Owned by a Parisian and his terse, blonde wife, Christophe's baguettes were perfectly crunchy on the outside and with just the right amount of chew on the inside. I'd often pop in after a morning run, lingering in the cool shop after selecting a baton to soak in the smells of espresso and savory sandwiches while watching shopgirls whisk chocolate into steaming cups of milk. Romantically painted myself into this scene, I rejoiced one November morning when an advertisement for seasonal help appeared in the shop. I applied on the spot and was soon tying a black apron behind my back as I stared at rows of chocolates behind a glass counter. Vanilla Bean Dark Chocolate, Mango Rum White Chocolate, and Lemon Milk Chocolate: their fragile dustings and tiny embellishments were as complex as their listed flavors and I wondered why any human would bother with cheap, plastic chocolate. The very idea of biting into one of these chocolate's silky insides sent a thrill down my spine.

My mind jolted to attention as a stout hiring manager outlined my task. "I'd like for you to arrange twelve pieces of chocolate into an eye-catching display. A correct mixing and matching cannot, I'm afraid, be taught," she asserted. "One can either design chocolate boxes or one cannot!" Taking a breath, I reached forward to pick up a gold dusted octagon and cautiously placed it into the box. Gazing at the manager and back at the chocolates, I next approached a two-toned milk and white chocolate shell and gingerly secured it beside the octagon. Detecting a slight nod of approval, a soft sigh released through my pursed lips. Two chocolates successfully in; ten more to go. The tension mounted as I selected one after another, knowing that any moment my vision of becoming a shopgirl would be lost forever.

The chocolate gods smiled upon me that day, however, and soon I was prancing home with a hint of praline lingering on my tongue. Envisioning myself as Audrey Hepburn, humming about the shop in matchstick leggings and ballet flats as I whisked chocolate and arranged chocolates, I could barely wait to retie my apron. Shortly before starting, however, I was compelled to decline my sweet offer due to a chance meeting with a popsicle seller who set my sights on a different path. Although I try to not regret past decisions, I occasionally wonder where I'd be now if I'd chosen the chocolatier path. Could I have settled into a rhythm as a shopgirl? Might I have learned to decorate exquisite truffles, married Cody, and driven to the beach for picnics on the weekends? Perhaps the next five years would have rolled out in a smoother fashion, but then again, what an adventure I would have missed...

～

Southern Ground is a two-day music festival drowning in southern spirit. Although I am far from a home-grown country girl, I was currently reveling in all things southern. This included exclusively listening to 92.5 Kickin' Country on the radio as I frosted strawberry cupcakes and dropped cookie dough in my tiny kitchen, or joined Cody on road-tripping adventures on bright Saturday afternoons. Consequently, the moment festival billboards popped up all over town and Kickin' Country announced that year's swoon-worthy line-up, I implored Cody to buy us tickets while I scouted out a pair of blue jeans and a cute plaid shirt.

The opening acts were well underway when Cody and I entered the Southern Ground fray, gussied up and ready to party country style. After ordering a hot platter of anxiety-inducing fries, we headed for the bleachers to whoop and holler with the best of them. As Nashville celebrities in white stetsons and spurs poured out their soulful hearts, a popsicle seller on the field below caught my attention. He was casually leaning against his cart and enjoying the show until a muddy pair of boots appeared from time to time to demand a banana puddin' treat. My curiosity peaked, Cody and I climbed down from the bleachers to investigate. How had he scored a spot selling popsicles today? Grinning with pleasure at our interest, he described an expedition with his buddies through the jungles of South America, their obsession with Spanish popsicles, and subsequent experimentations with every popsicle flavor imaginable. Fast forward a year and these guys were running a small frozen empire, sending employees with little carts to events all over the state. "Why couldn't we do something like this?" I asked Cody.

A few days after Southern Ground, Cody and I drove out to Sullivan's Island. While its neighboring beaches Folly and Isle of Palms are flooded with sun-worshippers during the summer months, "Sully's" remains serene. Sturdy wooden planks, flanked on either side by untamed ocean reeds, lead to a long and wide beach that is #nofilter stunning. Ocean-swimming humans are typically few in number, but impeccably groomed golden retrievers and fleets of mini sandpiper birds are easy to spot darting in and out of the waves. My thoughts this evening were consumed not by pups or pipers, but by popsicles. Curating chocolate boxes was a charming vision, but the idea of owning a cookie company was enchanting. Here was a chance to create a beautiful existence as a poised and graceful business owner/hostess, racing about in heels and drop earrings to ensure each customer and a team of bakers felt enveloped in sugary happiness.

Cookies were an obvious choice. Sure, I loved immersing myself in forbidden desserts and vicariously biting into chocolate, but I believed my interests extended beyond my disorder. I'd dreamed of owning a shop for years; a retreat for women to enjoy blissful moments in a space decorated with seasonal florals and pretty rustic-chic tables and chairs. Although I questioned my worthiness to enjoy such respites, I felt other women deserved to press pause on their busy lives. A business plan and six original recipes were already waiting in the wings. With Cody's business-savvy brain, I was determined we could create a polished and sustainable company, first as a portable enterprise and then as an established brick and mortar brand. Cody's excitement matching my own, we brainstormed marketing concepts as the pups disappeared and darkness descended on the beach. Checking the time, we walked back over the planks and off the sand to duck into Home Team BBQ for a helping of brisket, biscuits, collard greens, and giddy chatter.

18

MARATHON TRAINING IN CONVERSE

CHARLESTON, SOUTH CAROLINA: AGE 30

Trey was a husky wedding caterer with a mess of shaggy hair and a great hound that followed him everywhere. His reception venue was nestled between a corner shop and a dog park on the north-side of King Street, where a sprinkling of hipster eateries breathed new life into an area dominated by dilapidated homes and scruffy stray cats. Situated amongst this complex grit, Trey's venue was surprisingly elegant. Mini strings of magical white lights flooded the patio with a soft glow. Rows of hefty oak tables decorated with hurricane candles provided a modern, farmhouse charm. A scent of fresh herbs, buttermilk biscuits, and spiced chicken attracted reception guests entering like moths to a fluorescent light.

We were lucky to find Trey. Digging our cookie aspirations, he kindly gave us a free-run of his mixer and ovens whenever he wasn't prepping for an event. Consequently, although his kitchen oozed a Sorcerer's Apprentice atmosphere, with a sink often heaving under the weight of party plates, I was too excited to work in a pro kitchen to care. Pushing in my ear-buds on my first day, I turned up Harry Connnick Jr.'s jazzy "Come By Me" while organizing Nestlé chip bags into stacks. Then, apprehensively eyeing a commercial Hobart mixer in the corner, I got busy. My right arm moved like a dancer, whisking in quick motions and drawing wide circles with a wooden spoon, as Harry and the Hobart grooved and whirled in the background.

Liberal vanilla pours, golden hued sugar merges, and clouds of flour incited my senses as I batched and baked my way into the afternoon and the following week. Finally, after endless variations of my recipes, mini bakes emerged from the oven looking Bon Appétit cover worthy. But the taste? Brimming with hope, I carefully inserted my best looking efforts in Ziplocs, marked each bag with a black Sharpie, and rang Cody. "Can you pick me up? I think tonight's the night! How do you feel about cod and sautéed squash for dinner?" Cody seared fish while I seared samples into razor thin slices for testing. Creating a romantic cookie mood post flaky fish, we lit candles, poured two stemmed glasses of water as palette cleansers, and bit into sweetness. Calling out subtle textures and flavor nuances like experienced sommeliers, we narrowed down our favorite varieties until, leaning back into soft cushions, we declared our cookies worthy of a coming out party on the Carolina stage.

We rapidly sold cookies by the dozens and then by the hundreds, with holiday celebrations, farmers markets, and music festivals fueling our operations until we could afford to open a downtown Charleston shop. Consequently, after securing a larger kitchen space across Charleston's iconic Cooper River Bridge, I signed us up for popular events across the state while Cody formulated baking quotas. On the eve of an event, Cody and I arrived at the kitchen—me in a white tank, Converse, and tight ponytail—ready to make cookie magic. After removing hundreds of cookie dough balls from a walk-in freezer, we'd spin, twist, slide, lift, and flip fifty professional sheet pans for six hours at lightning speed to ensure a consistent cookie quality at 325 degrees F. Until we perfected our process, a 1000 count bake often ended in tears as I realized we'd forgotten to remove trays of Peanut Butter Cookies out of an oven or that we'd hastily set the temperature to 375 degrees F; either of which resulted in the discovery of charred cookie brittle. Regardless, our cookies were eventually cooled, sealed, and frozen for fresh keeping until the following morning. After a late night feast at The Shelter, our go-to burger joint, I'd toss in my duvet with heartburn and anticipation until I drifted into unsettled dreams of crowds clamoring "Cookies! Cookies! We want cookies!"

~

I wandered into our kitchen at dawn, slipping on a pair of scratchy mittens while locating a large key. Cody was parked around the back and opening our trunk when I appeared with the key to open the outside walk-in freezer. Once the cumbersome lock was removed, I pulled back the door to flood the darkness with a bright light. Cody's brother Jack had recently joined our cookie enterprise and I was grateful for extra hands as we crammed frozen product into our SUV. Working quickly, I yanked out a last cheeky Tupperware hiding behind a box of chicken breasts before popping back into the kitchen to fill large urns with water. As Cody and Jack heave-hoed our tent and tables through the trunk, I grabbed canisters of Swiss Miss, tablecloths, and business cards to squeeze into any backseat crevices. Then, like an ice cream truck packed with treats, we zoomed to the Charleston Marathon finish line, weaving around coned off areas until we arrived at our allocated vendor space.

Hitting the marathon circuit was a gamble, but after accumulating $2,500 in cookie sales the past two days at the race expo, I arranged our booth with controlled optimism. My restraint was due to this morning's wild card weather. The sun was now high in the sky, but the temperature remained a bitter thirty-seven degrees F with fifteen mph winds. Fearing all sales might be lost as I eyed our frigid cookies, I drowned my sorrows in shots of hot chocolate. As a sugar rush propelled manic jumps into the air to improve my circulation, however, a crowd began beelining towards our "Cocoa Sold Here" sign in search of warmth. Giddily, Jack handed cookies to customers while I sold cups of hot chocolate faster than Cody could boil enough water. Intently following their cup's journey through the line, customers bit hard into cookies, relaxing their shoulders down and back as saliva softened the dough enough to swallow. Suddenly, my eyes flitted from our queue to a thickset woman in a pink zip-up and neon blue shorts commanding my attention.

"I'll take a cup of chocolate please, and, uh, one of those oatmeal ones!" she announced.

"Absolutely!" I chimed back. "That will be five dollars. Thanks so much and well done on your race!"

She reached into her hot pink zip and then looked back at me with childlike despair. "I can't move my fingers! Would you mind reaching into the back of my sports bra? My card's in there!"

She couldn't have asked a more willing business owner; I understood the panic of realizing food is beyond your grasp when you can almost taste flavors on your tongue. Quickly inserting a cold hand down her back, I fished a Visa out of her strap as Jack produced a steaming cup and cookie. I furtively watched as she walked a few paces off and leaned forward to breathe in Swiss Miss' nostalgic aroma. Taking generous bites of cookie between sips, she looked about the finish area with a contented smile. There was no rush; no glance at a watch or calculated body check. There was only self-love—a moment to soak in feelings of accomplishment in the company of cocoa and a cookie. Once a final bite was polished off and her cup tossed into a nearby bin, she leisurely inhaled a breath of air and scurried back into the chaos of proud mothers, missing family members, abandoned orange slices, and frigid humans clad in tinfoil capes and brass medals. Our fleeting encounter left a permanent mark on my heart. Although I was bundled in somber gray layers and hardly radiating hostess vibes, this woman in pink personified my original business objective to create blissful moments for women, which I might also deserve at some point. Paying her spirit forward in the ensuing hours, I surrendered my usual sales obsession to share laughs with customers and to pass free cups to racers separated from their wallets. In Grinch-like fashion, my heart grew three sizes that morning as I mused that simple connections and small pleasures—rather than tangible results—might just be the best part of life.

SELF-LOVE GEM: PRACTICE THE ART OF SELF-CARE

I hope your childhood was full of bubble baths, freeze-tag, hugs, cupcakes, and satisfying meals. As busy adults, we often feel too busy to sleep and view baths or treats as gratuitous luxuries. Many of our needs, however, mirror those of children; sleep, nutrition, and pleasure are all key components of excellent mental health. Self-care is a broad concept centered around treating yourself kindly each and every day. Manifestations include reframing negative thoughts, giving yourself space to breathe, focusing on what you did well rather than on what you did poorly, and accepting compliments. Thankfully, as you integrate self-care into your life and absorb its lasting benefits, you'll feel stronger, calmer, and happier. A bath, sleep, or a cupcake are not prizes to be won; rather, they are evidence you're treating yourself with the respect you deserve.

19

DON'T GO BACON MY HEART

CHARLESTON, SOUTH CAROLINA: AGE 31

The Myrtle Beach Marathon was the next stop on our marathon circuit. As expected on a bright, bluebird February 15th morning, we sold cookies like hotcakes to runners, spectators, and local celebrity Bubbles the Elephant, who gobbled a half dozen Peanut Butter cookies out of my hand. Wiping slobbery crumbs off cold mittens, I overheard a sweaty customer ordering Snickerdoodle Cookies declare to her husband, "These are the cookies I *always* get at marathons; they're the best!" On the surface, I was soaring on customer kudos and cookie profits. Under six layers of sweaters, however, my mental cookie was crumbling. Regardless of my true self's ambition to pursue balance, a distant dream justified a compulsion to push myself to the limit. I would treat myself kindly *once* we baked and sold millions of cookies. I could relax on a beach with a glossy magazine *after* we opened our shop in downtown Charleston. A beautiful existence with moments of sugary bliss was obtainable, but first I needed to achieve praiseworthy results.

Self-Love Gem: Savor happiness now

Although delayed gratification has its place, there's no need to sacrifice your well-being to achieve your goals! Rather, allocating time to rest, eat property, self-reflect, or to simply stare off into infinity are important ways to keep your mind fresh and your body strong. Take time to enjoy small pleasures, celebrate mini wins, and praise your efforts as you continue towards your lofty goals. Treating yourself with loving kindness from dawn to dusk will improve your chances of success and ensure you reap the benefits of healthy living that are scattered along your way.

Working my tail feather off was familiar territory; manual labor was not. Apart from lifting free weights at gyms, I'd rarely hoisted anything heavier than a crammed weekend tote. Now, like an ant carting frosted cupcake chunks from a picnic, I was hauling bags of flour half my body weight, turning over pounds of densely packed dough, boiling vats of water to soak raisins and cranberries, and shuttling Tupperwares in and out of freezers. After a Monday to Friday schedule of batching dough and a late night bake, we'd pack our frozen cookies and gear, to include sandbags to ground our tent, hundreds of miles to sell for twelve-hour stints. If the sun shone and the crowds heaved, I'd skip water and limit my intake to mini cookie bites to close every sale until, festive merrymakers few in number and a cold darkness falling, we'd call it quits. Stumbling into a local joint at 11:00 p.m., I'd scarf down a chicken sandwich and fries until my stomach swelled from the sudden injection of calories. Ruminating over this "failure" in a motel bed, I'd vow tomorrow would be different, but of course it never was. I might be ace at quelling an impending binge, but as a starving sales woman, sweet potato fries with a side of mayo didn't stand a chance.

Beyond kitchen acrobatics and ED endurance contests, cookies were a relationship killer. A "Don't take this personally!" from Cody was taken *very* personally and a "Maybe I should leave the voicemails for clients, Rach," sounded exactly like "You suck at leaving messages!" Dinner dates devolved into strategy sessions, company expansion plans bombarded moonlight walks, and intense conversations devolved into arguments that killed the last remnants of the dreamy southern mood we'd originally savored. Jack's arrival added an extra coating of stress to our relationship. He and I got along brilliantly, but stir in Cody and hello sibling confrontations! It was soon evident Charleston and cookie cash promises recruited Jack to our cause; not warm and fuzzy brotherly love. I hated their arguments, Jack's aggressive presence on dinner dates, and his insistence that Cody and I avoid any public displays of affection. Most maddening of all, Jack's Grand Slam breakfasts rocked my world. Bounding into the kitchen each morning, he'd light the fires to fry up seasoned chicken and ham, scrambled eggs and hash, onions, squash, beans, and yams. Standing strong against this onslaught of pungent aromas, I'd nibble on my buttered english muffin and pray the worst was over until bacon hit the pan. Once this happened—once my gut sensed a pig sizzling nearby—my ancestral food sensors went berserk.

Cue the hunger pangs! Cue the saliva! There's bacon in town!

As the powerful odor of pork belly consumed the house and my body trembled with bacon lust, I'd gather my laptop and chapstick, grit my teeth, and storm out the door to seek shelter in a nearby, sterile hipster coffee shop.

I didn't make life easy! A love junkie would have sustained her body on weekend escapades with wholesome wraps, nuts, and dried fruit. She would have sacrificed a few sales for the sake of hydration and bathroom stretch breaks, and spent the extra $30.00 on a firmer hotel bed with crisp, clean sheets. Secure and confident, she also would have requested Cody take her out alone periodically to ensure she felt special in cute heels and lipstick. She definitely would have spoken to Jack about her breakfast anxieties (while adding nut butter and bananas to her meagre muffins) and asked both gents to deal with their sibling issues elsewhere. Such actions would have certainly improved my standard of living and ebbed the swelling torment permeating through my body. Instead, by the time the Myrtle Beach Marathon rolled around, I was all around bacon-austed, with only vibrant customers and a flurry of cookie sales shoring up my sanity.

SELF-LOVE GEM: REFLECT ON WHAT YOU DESIRE

It's easy to sprint for days without looking up at the clouds or taking a moment to consider where you are at and where you are going. Pausing to consider your needs and priorities (and reshuffling your calendar accordingly) is an important act of self-care. What do you want your life to look like? What skills and attributes would you like to nurture? What are your short, medium and long-term goals? I was chasing cookie mansions in the sky when my true ambition was to open a small cookie shop. If I had slowed down to self-reflect, I might have designed a game plan that aligned with my dreams while accounting for my needs. Sure, sometimes we must manage affairs we don't love and didn't choose— sometimes life is just plain tough. By proactively assessing your motives and goals, however, you'll feel more in control of your life and better equipped to make smart decisions.

We packed up our booth and headed southwards to Cracker Barrel, *the* place to stop for chicken 'n dumplings on southern road-trips. I was happy to be warm, grateful for a morning of rapid fire cookie sales, and relieved buttermilk biscuits were on their way. As my sales adrenaline wore off, however, flashbacks of yesterday (a frigid dawn at the kitchen, a two-hour drive north, a tussle with Cody escalating into a cold war, and a Denny's stop) wrecked my vibe. My confidence tottering on a daily basis, a midnight Valentine's dinner at Denny's was by far the worst offense. As a gummy "Fit Fare" omelette arrived and Cody and Jack launched into their bacon-laced skillets, I wondered if my choices warranted this reality.

How did I end up in a Myrtle Beach Denny's with my boyfriend and his brother tonight? Will I ever feel like a classy and wanted woman on Valentine's? Everything feels wrong and I'm so tired; can I trust my choices at all? I feel farther from my dream shop and a kinder existence than ever before.

My flashback was suddenly interrupted by Cracker Barrel's roaring fire and the appearance of Brandon and his girlfriend, whose entrance emitted a rush of energy throughout the restaurant. "Hey guys!" Brandon called out, "Vanessa and I thought we'd surprise you on your way back to Charleston. I know the plan was to meet up tomorrow, but I was too excited to see my sister!" A cowboy at the table to our right seemed particularly miffed by this unexpected racket. Clearing his throat as we hijacked extra chairs and ordered Colas and sweet teas, he shot us a peeved glance and then stuffed another forkful of dumplings into his mouth. Just like Jack, Brandon and Vanessa were between chapters in their lives. Consequently, a few weeks before, Cody and I had arranged for them to join our party for a short-term cookie experience. I was elated; nothing could be finer than to have a best friend in town to break up our threesome and inject our kitchen with vibrant enthusiasm. Consequently, although I'd hoped for a hot shower, a snooze, and a date with my hair straightener before greeting my brother's girl, I stuck my straw into a large Diet Coke and, with relief, hoisted my crumbly spirits back onboard the happiness train. Today was the start of a new chapter in which a beautiful existence was once more possible.

20

A HOSTESS WITHOUT THE MOSTESS
CHARLESTON, SOUTH CAROLINA: AGE 31

Steaming towards cookie castles in the sky, I doubled our batching and baking schedules and committed our team to impending festivals in North Carolina and Georgia. Soon we'd be toasting our success on a warm and swanky rooftop patio, dancing in cocktail dresses and button-down shirts to honeyed southern tunes without a care from the top. What was a bit of elbow grease now? After loading Tupperwares and tables into a rental van, Cody and I wished Jack, Brandon, and Vanessa a "Good luck up there; let us know if you have any trouble!" and then sped towards Savannah, Charleston's party cousin to the south. I was a bit apprehensive about sending three strong personalities with 2,500 cookies to a multi-day event in the opposite direction. Having sorted every detail of their trip down to the last chocolate-chip, however, I was confident we'd soon reunite to share amusing stories over The Shelter's burgers and fries. Unfortunately, mayhem erupted up north as Jack clashed with Brandon and Vanessa over an intensive thirty-hours of sales, culminating in a stormy ride home and an all-out war upon their return that continued through the spring and into the early summer.

Vanessa was the most vehement of all, casting icy glares in my direction and persistently dumping her grievances to my brother. She'd expected a holiday of light work, beach parties, and fun, comped dinners; all of which she demanded align with her whims and preferences. Unhappily thrown by my workaholic kitchen rituals, she maintained a silent yet chilly haughtiness that cast a gloomy aura on the house and triggered a quick beating of my heart. Brandon, caught between a high maintenance girlfriend and a manic sister in an inexplicable cookie trance, condemned my unfair treatment of Vanessa and threatened to report my behavior to our family, the latter of which sent my fury into the stratosphere. Brandon also demanded Cody rein in his brother, since Jack was continuously demonstrating aggressive, bad behavior between batching cookies and frying up Grand Slam breakfasts. Although Cody occasionally confronted his brother, he was too proud to admit any management errors on his side. Rather than rising as the hero of the hour, Cody reinforced the chip on his shoulder and dismissed opportunities to smooth over tempers or to ensure team members felt properly valued for their work.

Taken en masse, our house was a tinderbox of sparks and explosive encounters as five people, all blindsided by their own perspectives, struggled to keep calm and cookie on. A storm of Mal chatter swelled in my mind as I maintained a grueling work schedule and attempted to mitigate team drama. Nursing burns from spinning hot pans, batching from dawn to dusk, and spending twelve-hour shifts on my feet, I lost my patience with attitudes and refused to pour out feigned kindness.

These people came to help us out! It's not time yet for celebrations. Why are they asking so much of me and making my life harder? Don't they understand what we're trying to achieve?

Dissatisfied, overwhelmed, and anxious, I dug in my Converse and attempted to just "get on with it", without realizing how much lovelier life might have been if I'd reduced our cookie commitments and treated us all to occasional Sully's beach outings and lazy daisy brunches overlooking the harbor.

SELF-LOVE GEM: MANAGE YOUR EXPECTATIONS

We constantly set expectations based on what we believe should happen in the future. We expect a hotel room to smell like fresh cotton, we expect a significant other to greet us with a smile, and we expect a stand-up comedian to elicit tears of laughter. The trouble is, we live in an imperfect world filled with imperfect people, to include ourselves. By setting high expectations without room for mistakes or unexpected events, we set ourselves up for disappointment. Likewise, without clarifying our limitations and desires, we risk the dissatisfaction of others. We can't dictate how friends, family, or coworkers react, but we can proactively express what we can and cannot give, and listen to others' needs and expectations.

I was exasperated and ready to pitch Vanessa out on her nose when she requested a team meeting in her room late one night. Plopping myself down on the carpet with my hair in a messy ponytail and my bare legs crossed, I anxiously awaited a hard-done-by lament. Sitting in a place of prominence on top of her bed, Vanessa launched into a public shaming of my character. She declared I was a dire manager, a dreadful business owner, and an awful host. "I would never dream of treating people the way you have..." she continued, but it was too late—

my brain was fixated on "awful host". This impactful phrase reverberated through my body as a fire rose from my toes into my lungs and heart, steaming into my throat and ears with such force that my airways short circuited and were completely cut off. As I gasped for breath and dilating pupils blurred my vision, the heat in my brain became so intense my ponytail nearly burst straight off the top of my head.

Out! I need to get out of here right this second!

I darted down the steps, threw open the door, and raced onto the street like a fire truck tearing down a highway. As angry tears transformed into violent sobs, I slowed near a streetlight and upturned my head like a wild dog wailing at the moon. After years of silent confinement, wasp-y bottles of hate, envy, and guilt broke through the confines of my body and shattered onto the pavement like millions of tiny pieces of glass. "It's not fair!" I yelled into the darkness with melodramatic flair. "I hate them! I hate them all! I've done everything for everyone and tried my best to be perfect. I don't want to try anymore; I don't want to be alive anymore!"

Strong arms caught my narrow shoulders from behind as I sent my arms flailing upwards and my tears coursing downwards. "Rachel! Rachel Stop! Stop Rachel! Stop right now!" After an initial moment of frenzied resistance, I crumpled into Brandon's arms, weeping into his gray tee until I was worn out like a small child after a tantrum. "You're okay Rachel. You're safe and everything is going to be okay." Brandon's reassurances were a soothing balm to my wounded heart. The summer had strained our close friendship. We each felt the other was in a hateful relationship destroying their awesomeness and we were disappointed in one other. In the streetlamp's glow, however, family ties superseded our perspectives and expectations of one another. Bonded through a lifetime of shared experiences, Brandon knew my heart and loved me unconditionally. He knew how hard I'd worked to be the perfect sister, girlfriend, daughter, student, teacher, business owner, and hostess. Like Shawn and my parents, Brandon would always be there when I needed him the most.

As the quiet street came into focus and we wandered back to the house together, a sorrowful despondency overpowered familial comfort. Arranging city tours and hard to get reservations, creating curated, printed-out itineraries, and stocking my apartments over the years with pretty wrapped soaps, fluffy towels, and carefully frosted cakes and cookies, I'd attempted to radiate a version of my mother as a model hostess. My entire business model was based around a belief in my hosting prowess and a desire to make others feel appreciated, valued, and happy. Vanessa might take the intolerable visitor cake, but maybe she was right.

Perhaps I have failed as a hostess. And if I am a bad hostess, I must therefore be a bad woman.

I walked into the house as a self-proclaimed failure. My brittle cookie mixing back was broken and my true self silenced as if by a powerful enchantment. Without the hope of a prince or antidote to break the sorrowful spell, I slipped on a mask to shield my pain and hoped I might one day be happy again.

∾

Feeling gritty sand underfoot, I watched as mini sandpipers continued about their business, skirting along the water's edge as a humid breeze glided through the heavy air. I was relieved by Jack's, Vanessa's, and Brandon's departures and grateful to be once more barefoot with Cody on Sully's Beach. Although a sandy reprieve was satisfying, however, as spring gave way to summer and cookie madness continued, heavyweight questions tied to self-hate and food rumination plagued my battered mind.

Am I still in love with Cody? Can I ever marry him? If I stay in this relationship, will I ever be settled in a coastal home filled with joy and laughter?

Can I repair my relationship with Brandon and assume all guilt for our spring spectacle? Can I break up with Cody— a guy my brothers believe is a horrible person—without resenting them both forever?

Am I making my parents' lives miserable? Will they believe I am a good person if I don't immerse myself in religious devotion to live as they live?

How can I reconcile my family's and boyfriend's wishes with my feelings? Will I ever be truly happy again? Will I ever be good enough?

As I deliberated these questions on a minute-by-minute basis, I closed my eyes to envision a narrow shard jutting out from a sheer cliff. Standing in a silky gray dress with bare toes peeking over the edge, I feared I might topple over in an instant and fall to my death in the racing waters below if I could not immediately reach clear decisions. With zero trust in myself, however, I remained on this precipice, anxious to find a pathway down but paralyzed by internal deadlock. Mal took advantage of my torment to declare starvation my last hope. Intensive restricting would ease my pain and calm my heart like a familiar hug in a frightening world. If I could achieve a true lightness of being, as I'd experienced in Vancouver years before, I could once more confidently make decisions, reclaim control over my body and mind, and harness a lasting happiness. Swallowing this rotten proposal resulted in a heightened gnawing in my belly and violent attacks on my person. Regardless of how often I watched sandpipers along the waters' edge or how deeply I breathed into Jasmine petals on walks, mood swings, decision paralysis, comatose episodes, and racing thoughts disrupted scorching summer days.

Look how unhappy Cody is—I am responsible for making his life miserable. I wish I could escape everyone and everything forever. I want to disappear but my parents would be destroyed. I am not free; I am trapped.

I turned to obsessive cookie batching to numb my feelings. Creaming butter and sugar, turning batter over and over again, scooping dough onto cookie sheets, and creating tidy rows of rounded dough balls, I batched for hours like a possessed woman until, one excessively hot afternoon, I collapsed in sobs over our mixer. Dropping a heavy bag of cranberries to rush over, Cody led me outside and quietly drove us to the harbor. I felt his arm about my shoulders as we silently sat together on a park bench. Cody looked into the distance while tears rolled down my face and mingled with beads of sweat. Small white boats moved through calm water at a leisurely pace. A few children merrily laughed on a nearby swing set. Cody finally spoke first. "I think it's time Rach. We have to do something. I don't know how to help you anymore—this is beyond me." We were in agreement. Tossing my white flag onto the field, I held Cody's hand to walk back to our SUV, desperate to remove this heavy burden from my soul in a far off place.

SECTION VI: A BRAVE MOUSE NEEDS HELP

21

A BRIEF INTERLUDE OF NUTTY BUDDY THERAPY

VANCOUVER, CANADA: AGE 31

And now you find me right where we left off at the start—a hot mess whose just filled her belly after a seriously sweaty yoga class in Vancouver's trendy Yaletown.

~

Hot chicken breast, melted swiss cheese, mushrooms, caramelized onions, and spinach jostled in my belly as my ponytail whipped in a sharp wind. The chill felt good against my toasty core and I welcomed the feeling of sore abs against my jacket. Hot yoga was nearly unbearable, but an icy eucalyptus towel and tired muscles more than compensated for my sweaty pig pain. It was nearly 9:00 p.m. as I walked across the Granville Bridge and followed the street lights to Courtney's apartment. Courtney was a long-time family friend I'd met years before while working downtown with James. As a generous and kind spirit, I immediately sent her a quick message once I realized finding solace at my gram's house was a pipe dream:

Hey Courtney! I'm in town for a few months and would love to see you. I'm currently staying in White Rock, but my fam is visiting and I need some space; are you interested in a short-term roommate? XO Rach

I'd frequently daydreamed of returning to Canada, a place I associated with feelings of safety, belonging, freedom, and love. Consequently, after quietly watching the boats on Charleston's harbor, I researched therapists on Vancouver's Psychology Today website. Typing into the search bar phrases like "unable to cope" "anxiety meltdowns" and "complete disaster", I stumbled across Dr. Daryl, whose profile ticked all the right boxes. Crossing my fingers his skills matched his impressive credentials, I booked a month of biweekly sessions, left Cody in charge of our business obligations, and flew westward with hope and a White Chocolate Cranberry cookie in my purse.

~

I wore a sour expression as I bit into a very different kind of cookie thirty hours later. My Gram's biscuit-styled cookie was delicious and highly preferable to the bran muffins I'd expected to see in her tin, but discovering my brothers and sis-in-law were also en route to Canada was alarming. Was this an intervention? I was hardly surprised. My family hadn't attempted to mask their delight when I announced my intention to book therapy sessions in Vancouver. My mom had praised my good sense and promptly wired money into my checking account to cover Dr. Darryl's expenses. My brothers, adamant the three C's (Cody, Charleston, and Cookies) were responsible for my downfall, had advised I stay in Canada a few months, a year; forever! I found their pronouncements insensitive and unfair. Was my meltdown simply the result of two years in South Carolina, or was it based on perennial high standards, family pressures, hyper-productive habits, and an entrenched ED chomping away at my mental health?

It's a mash-up, of course!—I silently declared.

I will not be treated like an untrustworthy child without any understanding of my own brain! I will not be bullied by my family!

Unable to recognize Shawn's and Brandon's genuine concern for my health, I bolted into the city the moment Courtney accepted my proposition. September and October were disastrous. Between sunrises at Courtneys and sunsets at hot yoga, I could not keep it together. Even on stunningly gorgeous days, with red and gold maple leaves dancing in the wind on their downward trajectories, uncontrollable tears stained my cheeks on a packed SkyTrain or in the middle of a yoga class. Racing out the doors with embarrassment, a cold wind dried my face as I wandered city streets in a haze, questioning my purpose and comparing myself to Vancouver's most striking Sylvias.

Why can't I be one of these beauties dashing off to a well-paid job or a date at a trendy bistro? Why am I weaker than all of these women and unable to cope? And why did I eat banana bread this morning! Can I ever be trusted to make good decisions? Will I ever be good enough?

SELF-LOVE GEM: IMMENSE YOURSELF IN LOVE

It's easy to become susceptible to self-sabotaging behavior when we hit rock bottom. Too exhausted to fight negative thoughts, we accept the worst perspective of ourselves. What can you do in such circumstances, when it's hard to lace your sneakers, much less seize the day? You can choose love over hate by practicing self-care. Feeding yourself wholesome eats, stepping into nature, lighting a pumpkin spice candle, or sweating out stress in a spin studio can uplift the most depleted of spirits. Above all, resist the urge to isolate! Instead, reach out for love and support; assume that friends and family are there for you, just as you would be there for them.

Sporadic hip-hop classes and vanilla layer cake dates with Courtney kept my pitching and rolling boat afloat. Additionally, although I was self-isolating, an occasional family reunion downtown replaced manic and depressed thoughts with laughter and happiness. As my brothers took me out for sandwiches and walks around Vancouver's Seawall, I recognized their love and concern as my siblings and closest, lifelong friends. Perhaps I was less judged than I felt? Regardless, as the weeks passed by, I donned a pair of rose-colored glasses that cast an idyllic light on Charleston. I missed the scent of Cody's cologne as he leaned in for kisses, sunset walks and BBQ brisket at Sully's Beach, and authentic connections with strangers on cookie expeditions across the south. Anxious to justify a swift return home, I sweated my heart out in yoga classes, devoured the self-help section at a downtown bookstore, and arrived at therapy sessions ready to bare all.

~

Walking briskly in an early November breeze, I stopped into Whole Foods for a Nutty Buddy smoothie and peanut butter pretzels. As a blender vigorously hummed in the background, I stretched my yoga limbs this way and that and wondered if today was the day I'd discover the secret to happiness. Sticking a thick straw into my Nutty Buddy and squirreling my PB pretzels into my purse, I trotted back into the cold morning air. Twenty minutes later I was fifteen floors up and setting my empty cup on Dr. Daryl's coffee table. Looking at green bits of kale and banana stuck to the sides, I wished I'd taken an extra moment outside to locate a bin. I also regretted the pretzel forays into my purse on the elevator ride up. Concentration was essential this morning and now a reel in my mind was hell-bent on playing my elevator pretzel popping on repeat. Softly sighing, I nestled into a black leather couch and looked into Daryl's rectangular frames.

Soft-spoken and classically handsome, Dr. Daryl's conservative glasses capped off a starched yet unmemorable chino and button-down ensemble. He excelled at those "I understand you, keep talking" verbal cues like "hm-hmm" and "uh-huh, yes..." and shook out my tears with statements like, "You're an intelligent woman with two graduate degrees. Why don't you deserve to be treated with respect?" While I appreciated his validation and insights into my perfectionism, however, what I wanted was answers! How could I change? How could I rip the devil out of my brain to exude chill and lovin' vibes? Consequently, as he sipped his tea and inquired into my current emotional state, I launched into my recurring vision.

"It's terrifying at the top of the precipice, staring down at the rocks and racing water below! My life decisions must be settled soon, today even—otherwise I'll die from the stress of decision paralysis.

"The trouble is, I can't be trusted to make decisions; I can't even make the right breakfast choice! Perhaps I should do exactly as my family says—leave Cody, move to California, attend church, take a simple job—and try to not resent them forever, which I surely will do!

"Without answers, I dream of disappearing under my floorboards or running away to a small island where I can vanish forever. But I can't run away because it would break my parents' hearts. So, you see, I'm stuck in this reality and must make decisions I cannot make."

"Hmm. You're under a lot of pressure, Rachel," he quietly responded before taking another sip of tea. "But why must every question be solved today? Perhaps you need to ride out life a bit more to connect with your emotions and desires. Maybe now is the time to find comfort in the discomfort." I stared into his frames, stunned by this concept.

Find comfort in the discomfort.

It was such a simple idea, but the weight of these words infiltrated every cavity of my brain like a vibrant, psychedelic experience. Why couldn't I move forward without first requiring every piece of my puzzle to fit neatly into place? I couldn't make everyone happy all the time! Aspects of my world might remain in limbo for months; years even—and maybe this was okay. Perhaps uncertainty was an essential feature of life to embrace rather than to struggle against. If I kept my heart open and vulnerable the right decisions would eventually reveal themselves in illuminating ways. Yes, yes! I would find comfort in the discomfort and leap off my precipice to fly upwards into light, ethereal clouds.

An hour later I crossed the Granville Bridge to False Creek with my burdens lifted. A sharp nip in the air induced a quick shiver as I zipped my jacket to the tip-top and picked a park bench light on white splotches as a resting spot. Anxious to supplement my mental euphoria with other liberating gems, I fished Alan Singer's *The Untethered Soul* out of my purse. Like the rest of my accumulating self-help collection, I'd chosen Singer's book because of its alluring cover: an unbridled unicorn galloping alongside a deserted shoreline on a pretty aqua and gray background. I wasn't sure of the symbolism, but I instantly wished to transform into this silky creature, free of restraints and racing alone in a serene, natural setting without any foreseeable danger. Besides, who doesn't want to be a unicorn? Flipping to the Introduction, I silenced the world and tucked into the pages; it wasn't long before I stopped in my tracks, face to text with a profound concept:

"There is nothing more important to true growth than realizing that you are not the voice of the mind - you are the one who hears it."

At rare moments in our lives, a truth is revealed that propels our soul to leap with joy. "Yes!" it seems to shout from deep within us, "This is truth we've always known and that we can now manifest and celebrate!" Singer's statement was one of those moments. His assertion resonated with such a force that I closed the book to stare at my chipped red nails resting on his aqua and gray cover. It was true; it must be true! I'd fallen prey to a voice I'd always assumed was my own and now, after years of empowering her, my well-being was shattered. I abhorred my compulsion to starve and work myself ragged in the name of perfection; I wanted to be like Café Primo Sylvias, or the woman in pink chillaxing with a cookie and cocoa after her race. Moreover, I'd always believed in the pit of my gut that I am a kind and sweet human who values connection, acceptance, and a satisfied belly. Now I knew the truth: the voice in my head was not my voice and goodness lay within me, ready to break free. After running riot for fourteen years in my brain,

Mal was finally exposed as a destructive villain. I would still continue to honor her desires in the future, at times too weak or confused to resist, but in this moment I unwittingly took a huge step towards becoming an emancipated love junkie—I recognized my ED voice.

22

PINING FOR LOVIN' VIBES
CHARLESTON, SOUTH CAROLINA: AGE 31

Two powerful ideas can turn your world around. Racing thoughts abated as I stopped wrestling with my problems and recognized cruel thoughts as an external force. Cake and hip-hop classes with Courtney morphed into fun, girly activities and downtown dates with Shawn and my sis-in-law became highly-anticipated events. Most remarkably, a burden lifted as Brandon and I surrendered our pride to forgive each other for our roles in the Charleston drama. Once more loyal friends who saw and believed the best of each other, we climbed to a favorite viewpoint in a seaside village and bit into luscious donuts at a locals spot down below. We breathed in the salty air at our gram's beach to channel our childhood ghosts, shared our plans for how to move our lives forward, and arranged future sibling adventures on both coasts. As the weeks rolled by more gently, and despair and anger transformed into hope and understanding, I became unstuck; I stopped living in the past and fearing the future to bear-hug the present with open arms.

The present soon became Charleston. I returned home on a high, convinced my comatose episodes, bursts of acute anger, and deep periods of depression were done and dusted. The first two weeks were stunners. Sully's sunsets shone more vividly than ever before, I was shipping cookies across the country with a pep in my step, and Cody and I couldn't keep our hands off each other. But then, all too quickly the bloom fell off the violets and I relapsed hard, stricken by toxic emotions I'd expunged in Vancouver. What went wrong? A sliver of light was now in my heart, shining truth outwards in sharp golden rays. Although I was repairing my sibling relationships and offering myself more grace, however, true healing requires an enormity of patience and time. More importantly, while therapy, hot yoga, and hip-hop classes are all tasty medicine, at my core a skinny anorexic rhino was still unabashedly pirouetting in my mental kitchen. From restricting, binging, and ruminating to self-loathing, hyper-producing and irrational goals, anorexia had twirled for over a decade. I might passionately hate my ED voice and crave a kinder existence, but until I acquired the right tools, I could not race down a path towards Recovery and rectify the dichotomy of my life: a belief in my soul that *I am good enough* and a belief in my brain that *I am not good enough*.

It's hardly surprising, then, that once I returned to a manic company schedule and ran smack into new anxieties, Mal flexed her muscles to destroy my Vancouver mojo. Relationship tension swiftly became the bitter cherry on top of cookie stress. I was accustomed to bickering with Cody, but a meltdown can really kill your stamina for arguments. Subtle yet snarky remarks about my family left sour aftertastes that inevitably erupted into convoluted battles by the end of which, confused and exasperated, I'd fall apart and accept all blame. For a woman replete with self-hate issues, these unsatisfying episodes marginalized my emotions and strained my weak spirit. I couldn't understand why it was so hard; why couldn't we just make up and be happy? Since we could not, however, calling it quits became an increasingly alluring prospect. At first I resisted this solution. I loved Cookies, I loved Charleston, and I loved Cody! In my heart, however, I was no longer "in love" with my three C's and, consequently, a few months later Cody and I were finding a loving home for our Hobart mixer and filling gallon-sized Ziplocs with cookies to spirit away on our upcoming, solo adventures.

On my last day in South Carolina, Cody drove us through torrential rain to the airport. As the rain beat against the terminal windows, I weeped with anguish. More than any other goodbye, this one was the hardest. This wasn't how my story was meant to go! I was meant to live in a coastal home as a happy wife and successful cookie shop owner/hostess. Now I was flying alone as a destroyed woman without a career, man, or place to call home. As I comforted my aching soul with a White Chocolate Cranberry cookie, I recalled a story about two mice who fall into a pot of cream. While one promptly accepts his fate and dies, the other works so furiously to escape he unexpectedly churns the cream into butter and climbs out. Could I ever mimic this brave mouse or would I continue to struggle until I gave up completely?

∼

Brandon was working at Nike's Oregon headquarters and if I aspired to emulate the brave mouse, I knew I needed support. With luck, I'd be employed *somewhere* soon and reclaiming the flickers of happiness I'd felt in Vancouver. In the interim, I booked a sublet in Portland's hipster-cool Pearl District replete with health stores, yoga studios, and micro-breweries. I felt like a better woman just walking through the doors of my new home. The inside emitted a calming, white cleanliness. A light scent of paint mixed with botanical candles intensified this heavenly aesthetic and, as I curled up for the night in a fresh duvet and listened to sparrows chirping outside, I dreamed of holding onto this feeling forever.

The following morning, I grabbed my purse and rushed outside to join Brandon for a siblings excursion. Rolling down our windows in jeans and baseball hats, we followed the Columbia River eastwards towards the Hood River Valley. As we reminisced about past road-trips together, I admired wild-flower clusters framing the freeway, their pinks and purple hues matching the Morionberry and Huckleberry milkshake adverts we passed on our route. Soon we were ascending into the mountains and watching the outside temperature drop. Like a happy pup with two tails, I stuck my head out the window to inhale the Peppermint Pattie freshness of towering pines. We continued to gain altitude until, at nearly 6,000 feet, we parked at Timberline Lodge to immerse ourselves in the sights and sounds of our pasts.

Patches of snow (unaware it was late May and time to melt) coated rich dirt underfoot as our cold feet snapped twigs and our fingers touched frigid creek water moving calmly about its business. A spiritual reawakening washed over my body in the shade of pines that allowed just enough sunlight to peek through their boughs to keep us warm. Home was an elusive concept I'd captured in Vancouver, Los Angeles, and Charles-ton, but Mount Hood eclipsed all these connections. Chopping trees worthy of gold tinsel, riding up ancient tow-ropes in a marshmallow parka, hiking with candy bars stowed in our pockets for a treat, and camping out under the stars in the summer: Oregon held the key to childhood joy and in my brother's company I felt as rooted to this earth as the young firs in sight. Back off the mountain, we stopped into Portland's Salt & Straw for a late afternoon cone. As we waited in the queue to sample their Birthday Cake & Blackberries flavor, I imagined my gram swirling blackberries and cream into a luscious milk-shake. I also recalled gleefully ordering a scoop of Rocky Road with Brandon while sugar cones baked in the distance. Ice cream held a complicated place of love and binging in my heart, but today I honored love with a split-scoop of Honey Lavender and Sea Salt with Caramel Ribbons. Savoring the cold sweet-ness on my tongue, my thoughts turned to the brave mouse. Yes, I would churn my cream into something just as sweet and delicious.

Unfortunately, without the proper tools and with Brandon working full-time at Nike, Portland became a Charleston copy-cat. The views from cheerful coffee shops were different, but the racing thoughts and depressed emotions were identical. I attempted to avoid mini meltdowns, winding my way past thousands of velvety blooms in Portland's Rose Gardens and hiking through an expansive urban park. The moment stillness replaced movement, however, I craved the darkness and the escape it offered within the folds of my duvet. This cycle repeated until I face-planted on my bedroom floor one after-noon over a swiss and avocado bagel sandwich. On the heels of a Honeycrisp and glass of almond milk, I'd felt secure licking toasty crumbs until a snotty Manhattanite chick at a company breakfast a decade before upset my apple cart. Who knows how Mal pulled her from a deep layer of brain cache? Suddenly, however, she was at the forefront of my mind in a light pink cardigan, black pencil skirt, and knee-high boots. "One of those equals six slices of white bread, you know!" she smugly announced in a pinched-nose voice as a younger version of myself bit into a Cinnamon Raisin variety. I hated her then and I hated her now—even though my rational brain knew her statement was absurd.

It's more like three slices, you nitwit memory! Besides, it totally depends on the brand; this was a skinny bagel; totally safe and immensely satisfying.

Regardless of my bagel savvy and an awareness that I am not the voice in my head, I spent the next hour cheek to floorboard. A tortured creature, I could not resist sensations of failure, regret, despair, and disgust pulsing through my brain; my suppressed, true self was too weak to combat Mal's tongue-lashing. Destroyed yet incensed by the injustice of my inner voice, my internal monologue assumed a crazed, dual character.

I can't live with this fullness; why did I eat both halves? Why didn't I eat cheese and avocado and skip the bagel? I want to die. I should have waited until dinner. I don't deserve dinner now.

I hate this! It's just one lousy bagel; who cares?! I shouldn't feel this bad. I don't want to feel this bad anymore. I want to be a normal woman and enjoy my food in peace.

Then I shouldn't have eaten that whole sandwich! I'm far too full. My belly is too big. I'll never eat a bagel again. If I didn't eat that sandwich, today could have been a good day.

This is so stupid! This is insane! I'm insane! I can't take this anymore!

~

So there I was—a mouse drowning in cream and angry as hell because I vehemently wanted to stand on top of sweet butter but could not grasp the art of churning my legs under the thick liquid below. Unaware that my salvation lay within, I continued to look outwards for hope, deluding myself that good company and fresh stimuli would set me back on a path towards happiness. Brandon was a short drive away, but Vanessa had recently moved in with him, and, jealous of our sibling friendship, she callously mustered all her manipulative powers to keep us from spending much needed time together. Cody, however, was all about reopening communication and soon we were rendezvousing in Portland to road-trip back to California. It wasn't a brilliant plan—I knew our relationship status peaked as friends—but I still cared for Cody a lot and we had the most incredible times together, so long as we were both on our best behaviors.

As we drove southwards along a jagged coastline, stopping off for DQ Blizzards and hikes through the Redwood Forest, my angst melted away. Gone were the afternoons of depression and panic! Away were racing thoughts and food rumination that sent me face-planting onto lacquered floorboards! If only the good vibrations I experienced at blustery, scenic vistas had continued once we reached California. But, of course, once our best behaviors and good intentions dropped off and the ensuing months rolled along in Portland and Charleston fashion, I found it increasingly impossible to keep it together.

SELF-LOVE GEM: FACE YOUR FEARS

Rather than seeking professional help in Portland, I convinced myself another new life would set my world right. Like most big issues, however, I could not shoo-fly anorexia away. Until I faced my disorder head-on and did the tough work, I was plagued by anxiety, depression, and a debilitating ED voice that became increasingly obnoxious over time. The thing is, facing our fears is liberating! Not only do we experience relief, but we can also witness an increase in our self-confidence and our optimism about the future; we can stop fear in its tracks. So, go for it! Throw off your covers and see what happens when you face your demons. I bet you'll feel stronger, braver, and more in charge of your life than ever before.

23

FINDING MY CENTER

LOS ANGELES, CALIFORNIA: AGE 33

Fast forward a year and Cody and I were wading through The Virgin River in Zion National Park. The weather was glorious, the water mild enough to be deemed "refreshing", and the sunlight streaming into The Narrows displayed the full splendor of the canyon. Unfortunately, however, Mal was on the warpath that weekend, barging into this celestial setting with hateful thoughts and relentless ruminations. One challenging dinner and one anxious breakfast later, Cody and I were traveling home from Utah, my eyes distracting a tense mind with the immense granite formations, spiny-tipped Joshua trees, and a wide open sky. As fast food options on blue exit signs became increasingly attractive, Cody stopped for lunch at an out-of-the-way cafe.

My heart fell as my eyes skirted up and down a chalkboard menu—there was no "easy answer" sandwich; I was doomed to fail today. "Can you pick for us? I can't decide," I mumbled, repositioning my sunglasses back onto my nose and heading across the way to locate a shady table. Cody arrived a few minutes later with two PB&J sandwiches on white bread.

Although I wasn't sure of the best option at this cafe, it was absolutely not a jelly donut disguised as a sandwich. An argument ensued and soon I stormed down the street, flopping onto a low curb and cradling my hot face in shaky hands. I had been here so many times before: wretched with tears in my eyes, a lump in my throat, and a stomach teetering between famished and gorged. I'd cursed Cody's lack of ED understanding, ruined holidays over ice creams and fried chicken, and wished sunny days away to once more feel a clean emptiness in my belly. Sure, the scenery changed, but the story was always and forever the same.

Enough, enough already. I can't do this anymore.

~

I'd truly believed my disorder was manageable; that by simply "trying harder" food blues would dissolve and leave behind a skinny and peaceful facade. On this PB&J afternoon, however, I finally admitted the truth: I was a woman in need of professional help. Reaching into my jean jacket to locate my iphone, an anxious right thumb googled "Anorexia Centers Los Angeles". Pages of results populated, with "RECOVERY" "ANXIETY" "TREATMENT" and "STARVATION" leaping off my screen like emblazoned fonts on a film trailer. For an instant, I panicked and moved my thumb to clear my browser history and delete my cache. But then a vision of the brave mouse entered into my mind and I boldly dialed a number near the top of the page.

"Good afternoon, how can I help?" a voice asked on the other end.

I froze. Anorexia was a taboo subject I avoided completely. Apart from my family and Cody, I'd kept my dirty secret close to my heart and avoided all mention of eating disorders, to include online articles. Images of emaciated bodies are heartbreaking and I was scared to discover all the ways I'd permanently damaged my body. Now that I was reaching out, however, reality could not be avoided; I must open frightened eyes and expose my truth.

"I have a lot of bizarre eating issues," I stammered. "I think I need help." There! The first words were out; I could do this.

"I'm glad you called, Rachel. Can you tell me why you're reaching out now?"

"I can't handle my life anymore," I confided to this stranger. "I'm a total mess and desperate to be a normal woman. My perspectives on food and life are debilitating, but I can't escape them. I want to be happy again."

"I appreciate your honesty. Can you provide insight into your disorder? It will help us ensure we connect you to the right kind of support."

After a tentative kick-off, my words flowed fast and steady, like a green garden hose after a kink is released.

"I don't trust myself to make decisions about food or life. I spend hours in grocery store aisles, paralyzed by choice. Regardless of my selections, I'm inevitably consumed by guilt after consuming anything and obsessively analyze what option would have been better.

"Conjuring up an imaginary plate every hour helps me judge whether I have eaten the right type and volume of each food group throughout the day. Regardless of any external factors, this plate determines whether or not it's a "good day"—it's usually not.

"I dream of swallowing a daily pill to sustain my life so that I can avoid food entirely, but I also crave cupcakes and cookies like an addict. Consequently, I feel like a failed anorexic and greedy pig who's always on the verge of binging herself into a beautiful oblivion.

"Most of the day I hate myself and fantasize about transforming into someone completely different. I want to simply eat my food, but I cannot bear fullness or mental assertions that I am out of control and weak. Consequently, relaxation is a rare emotion I feel when there is just barely enough in my belly to think and exercise."

The man's calm yet nondescript voice never wavered; I might have been renewing my car insurance or ordering a Kindle replacement. After running through all his questions and arranging a subsequent meeting with a caseworker, he wished me a pleasant afternoon and hung up. I was stunned, dazed, confused, tapped-out—and surprisingly pleased. Exposing just a snippet of my authentic and complicated self to a faceless man had felt good; really good in fact. For the first time in my life, I'd spoken with someone who specializes in eating disorders and who was unfazed by my shameful habits and emotions. Why had I waited so long? A few minutes later, I returned to the cafe where a frustrated Cody was keeping my uneaten lunch company. As I silently sat down and tentatively sunk my teeth into jammy sweetness, I wondered if maybe my next sandwich encounter would be an easier experience.

～

The subsequent days flew by at a dizzying pace. I'd lived with an ED for sixteen years, but once I involved the pros, treatment became an emergency. Less than twenty-four hours after PB&J rolled through my intestine, ED center caseworkers and my HR department were drawing up a short-term disability plan. Based on my mental health and weight, an intensive outpatient program was declared the best fit, which meant that rather than around the clock support, I'd come and go from my selected center each day. By the following Monday, I was driving to

Santa Monica and wondering if I'd fit in at my female-only institution or be branded the weird "mom" who should have moved past anorexia a decade before. Thankfully, mental health is having a moment on our global stage, but society's version of anorexia is still an emaciated girl in her teens. I might be wearing skinny jeans, but a nightly balanced dinner followed by a ritualistic cookie served a la Häagen-Dazs ensured I wasn't *super* skinny. As I turned into the parking lot, Mal continued to contest my right to receive help.

Maybe I'm a fraud! I'm not skinny enough and I'm not a complete wreck. Do I really deserve to be here or is this just another one of my giant mistakes?

And yet, I was here for a reason; I was willing to do any and all things to remove the cancer from my soul. I parked and walked inside an avocado colored building, taking note of a small atrium in the middle as I climbed two flights of stairs and arrived at a nondescript door with a black number on the front. Turning the knob, I held my breath and stepped into a wonderland. Well, at $1000 of insurance dollars a day for admission, I anticipated a wonderland. My imagination running away in its typical fashion, I'd envisioned luminous pearl chandeliers, oversized cashmere throws and modern bean bags, and a mini bar of Godiva truffles and Sprinkles cupcakes to tempt patients into devouring high calorie treats. Instead, the décor matched the earthy tones of the corridors, with a large brown sectional, depressed in the middle from years of wear, assuming a place of honor in the main room. Currently empty of butts, only a hodgepodge of backpacks and books, carelessly strewn across mismatched blankets, provided the evidence of patients. I would later realize ED centers intentionally keep their spaces modest to hinder girls from perpetually dwelling in the arms of therapy. At first sight, however, I was ready to race right back out the door to drive my petite heinie back home.

Locking eyes with a young receptionist, however, I accepted it was too late to turn back now, and accepted a clipboard and a pen decorated like an oversized pansy. After returning the form and flower, she led me into the principal psychiatrist's office to wait for our introductory meeting. My skepticism skyrocketed as my eyeballs alighted on candles, figurines, and other spiritual kitsch, as well as a collection of mismatched frames that featured the doctor kickin' it back with the Dalai Lama and other faith leaders.

You have to be joking. I need real help! What does a guy in his sixties know about my pain? Will I be forced to consume a mountain of white dumplings and green tea while monks in orange robes lead us through hours of useless chanting? Ugh, why do I always rush into things!

A minute later the doctor arrived radiating a gentle and warm demeanor. As he shook my hand with smiling eyes, he seemed to appraise my body and understand my sorrows. I immediately felt like a judgmental dirtbag and reinstated my confidence in the center's ability to heal a broken woman. After outlining his extensive ED background and the center's philosophy that *complete* Recovery is possible, he inquired after my anxiety levels. Like a spooked horse calmed by a reassuring hand, I confided that I was terrified but prepared to give my best effort. Buoyed-up with reassurances and a wide smile, I left his office clutching a large binder of materials and feeling quite courageous.

SECTION VII: RECOVERY IS NO PIE IN THE SKY

24

BONDING WITH MY TRIBE

LOS ANGELES, CALIFORNIA: AGE 33

Three girls my age were eating lunch under the gaze of an attentive brunette. I took a seat at a floral placemat holding a Thai wrap and a homemade "Rachel" placard, and then looked to the brunette for guidance. "Welcome Rachel; we're excited to have you join us!" she chirped. "I'm Joy, a member of your treatment team, and this is Susan, Janet, and Natalie. We still have another ten minutes to enjoy lunch so dig in!"

I flashed a smile around the table, but my lunch-mates were far more preoccupied with their wraps than greeting a newcomer. Susan, a tough looking chick with scads of piercings, sat across from me in a loose muscle tank revealing an array of artistic tattoos. Leaning one painted arm onto the table, she was slowly drinking her way through a thick substance I would later identify as Ensure. Beside her sat Janet, who's current high meal plan had inspired her purchase of an over-sized Lululemon scarf to conceal excess belly weight. She glanced over at Joy like a mischievous child as she toyed with her wrap. Dipping its tortilla casing into peanut sauce, she lifted it up, and then submerged it once more into sauce before taking a small bite.

On my right sat Natalie, an attractive girl with dark features and a confident yet relaxed posture. Oozing LA chic in Rag & Bone boots and sassy DryBar blowout styles, our lifestyles were mismatched but our body types and mentalities were astonishingly sympatico. Starving on dates to feel sexy, picking pancakes over anything savory at brunch, and sweating out fevers in hot yoga? Yep, she did that too. Operating as functional anorexics for decades, Natalie and I had both ascribed to Kate Moss' 2009 statement that "Nothing tastes as good as skinny feels." Now we were both in therapy to transform this belief into something more like "Nothing feels as good as freedom from a toxic life."

I wasn't immediately in love with my ED twin. In fact, I hated Natalie immensely my first week as we attended sessions squeezed into our exhausting eating schedule. Sessions included illuminating the center with holiday decor, scribbling motivational letters to our future selves, pasting magazine clippings together to visualize our healthy ambitions, and brainstorming positive responses to our cunning ED voices. Most frequently, however, sessions involved arranging ourselves into a sloppy half-circle to kick it back in group therapy. My first encounter with this major aspect of center culture occurred after a hefty turkey taco lunch. Our treatment team leader that day was a surfer chick with a dolphin tattoo and an easy-breezy vibe. Like many center employees, she was a recovered anorexic who I esteemed as a symbol of hope in a challenging center world. After opening our session with a devotional message, she invited us to share our current emotional issues with the group, whereupon Natalie launched into a thirty-minute monologue.

"My mom's incessantly calling the center. I can't handle it;

my assigned therapist has called her twice already to set boundaries, but my mom sucks at boundaries. She keeps getting involved and it's driving me nuts...

"I've met this guy in AA who is cool and six months sober. I'm going to see him at another meeting tonight and think we could support each other, but I'm still hung up on my ex...

"I skipped my mandatory evening snack last night. I can't handle the idea of eating anything tonight. I've been freaking out about it since breakfast and I'm sure I'm going to fail again..."

On and on she raced, crossing her legs this way and that while nervously adjusting her Mai Tai blowout locks. I sat in disbelief, my thoughts oscillating between Natalie's tirade and an imaginary floating plate of tacos.

How can she still be talking? How can anyone yap this long to a group of women without coming up for air? What does this have to do with Recovery? I don't care! None of us care! And damn those tacos! I feel like a balloon ready to take flight. How am I going to down another snack in forty-three minutes? Ugh, this is such a waste of time.

Fidgeting in my chair, I wondered if the others were reeling from this insanity, but glancing in their directions, they appeared too drugged on meds or tryptophan to absorb the situation. I expected Janet would soon be snoring in the comfort of her grey Lululemon wrap, which was now functioning more as a blanket than a scarf. Our team leader spotted my wandering eyes and waved an aqua bangle in Janet's direction.

"Please stand up to shake off your drowsies! C'mon Janet, right this minute please! Perfect; thank you so much!"

Relieved by Janet's compliance, our leader smiled pleasantly around the room and recrossed one Rainbow sandal over the other. Janet yawned quietly as she stood up, like a sleepy cat forced to jump down from a comfy sofa. Once she stood upright, however, Janet jolted back to life; apparently, she'd been listening.

"You're all talk, Natalie! You clearly aren't going to eat your snack tonight! You never eat your snack and that's why you can't advance here. You get scared and make excuses.

"Also, your ex is lame and you need to let go. You vow to block him but then you let him back in and he tears you down. Sometimes it seems like you don't really want to recover."

I was stunned by Janet's bluntness. The room went silent as Natalie rested a manicured nail on the edge of her bottom lip. A few silent tears rolled down her cheeks. Tears are as common as chocolate-covered almonds in ED centers; I was on the verge of turning on my own waterworks from turkey taco fullness.

"Yeah, I know," Natalie finally responded. "He's one more addiction I struggle to let go of, but I am trying. You know I'm trying insanely hard, Janet! I am eating most of my snacks, and breakfast every single day."

It wasn't this afternoon. Today I was too fixated on tacos and my next snack in thirty-nine minutes to recognize the point of group therapy. A few mornings later, however, as I sat in LA traffic to spend the next twelve hours in an anxiety-inducing pressure cooker, its value smacked me squarely in the face. Far more than a treatment team, the center girls and I were a tribe in which piercings, race, hairstyles, and geography were inconsequential. We were super different, but each of us had reached a breaking point in our battles against a chronic disease and we were united in a common cause of salvation. We understood each others' pains, challenges, and heartbreaks better than anyone. The racing thoughts in my head mirrored Natalie's; I was just keeping them inside rather than exposing my feelings to receive support. The center offered hope, connection, and a release from mental anguish—why was I intent on going it alone?

I was ready when our next session rolled around, bravely expressing my fears and battling my emotions in real-time without allowing a reckless internal voice to call the shots. As I accepted honest feedback and called out others on their ED lies and skewed perspectives, Mal's commands and hateful commentary became less invasive and more irrelevant. I was slowly freeing myself from her clutches and learning to trust others and myself again. Don't get me wrong, I still hated the lunchtime tacos and my adrenaline skyrocketed as I faced each snack. But I no longer felt powerless and alone in my journey; rather, I was able to move bravely forward in the encouraging arms of strong women.

SELF-LOVE GEM: MOVE FORWARD, IN OR OUT OF A CENTER

Perhaps my center experience is directly relevant to your present situation. If you are considering admitting yourself to a facility or are already in sessions, take a leap of faith and go "all in"! Trust in the system and engage with your treatment tribe to receive as much strength as possible. If you can't attend a center or your challenges don't require professional help, my advice is the same: bravely prioritize your health. Rather than kick-starting a new diet or telling yourself you'll "try harder" tomorrow, reaffirm your dedication to self-love. This might involve setting aside time to prep nutritious lunches for the week, connecting with a social media support group, or walking with a friend to share your struggles and to offer one another support. Any step forward—no matter how minor—can meaningfully improve your well-being.

25

CHILI TEARS AND CHOCOLATE ALMOND FEARS

LOS ANGELES, CALIFORNIA: AGE 33

ED centers are like summer camps: within days I was immersed in the center's culture as a snack option expert and a kitchen rota duties master. As a newbie I was denied iPhone access and atrium breaks, and chaperoned to the bathroom to ensure I wasn't puking or pitching chocolate-covered almonds out a window. Thankfully, weekend field-trips into the real world, to include outings to West LA's hippest brunch spots, offset a lack of freedom and eased my center cabin fever. Our dietician Alice always led such ventures, which guaranteed a savory breakfast challenge proposal just as I was about to place a fruit parfait order. "Why not try the quinoa bowl instead, Rachel?" she'd innocently interject, knowing full well a jumble of eggs, broccoli, and onions at 9:00 a.m. guaranteed a paralyzing implosion that would last well into the afternoon. Still, sitting in a bustling cafe before the dreaded dish arrived always presented a sunny finale to a demanding week. Plus, no one could deny the tastiness of Gjelina's lemon ricotta pancakes or Huckleberry Cafe's scones that Alice would pass around as an appetizer.

The center's meal offerings were less desirable than Chocolate Hazelnut Scones. Similar to kiddie cafeteria flyers, meal calendars were circulated each morning for us to select our daily preferences. A particularly threatening meal could be swapped out for a PB&J sandwich, but doing so meant defending your choice to Alice, who encouraged us to face our fears not only in trendy cafes but also in our unassuming center kitchen. Consequently, just like Ensure (requested mid-meal when taking another bite became unthinkable), a PB&J lifeline was reserved for the most challenging dinners of all—like chili nights. Still on the rookie side of meals, I woefully accepted a gigantic bowl of ground beef, kidney beans, cheddar cheese, and sour cream one evening while Janet and Natalie munched on their substitute sandwiches. After a short stare-off with dozens of black kidney eyes, I dug a large spoon right into the middle.

This is all part of the process. I can do this. One bite at a time. Just a bit more and then a bit more; this will be over soon. Keep going; you are stronger than you think!

Digging deeper into thick redness, I continued on until a team leader stopped my feeding frenzy by asserting I'd finished my requisite amount that night. After the dishes were cleaned and table tidied, I stoically zipped my jacket to leave for the night. As I walked past the atrium and down the stairs, beef and cream tumbled about in my belly like a cauldron of acidic lava. The days were short now, and it was nearly pitch black outside when I walked to my car and flipped on the headlights. Merging onto the 405 with my window cracked for a hint of fresh air, I attempted to keep it together.

Just breathe; you're okay Rachel. In a few hours, all will be well. I'll skip tonight's snack and when I wake up this feeling will be gone. I will never eat another kidney bean in my life. It's over now. Be cool.

Self-care soothed my soul, but as molten chili churned at a fever pitch in my insides, it wasn't enough to subdue the panic pulsing through my body. Barely stepping across my apartment threshold, I watched in alarm as chunky slosh came hurling out of my mouth at full velocity, cascading through my tidy, beach home like a violent magma flow. Falling onto my hands and knees, I sobbed amongst my slop as I attempted to breathe in short gasps. Acid burnt my lungs and throat; floods of angry tears reddened my eyes and cheeks. Harkening back to my face-plants of yore, I longed to disappear forever under the cold floorboards currently holding my shattered body. Shattered, I slowly gathered myself off the floor, mopped up the rancid smells, and headed back out into the darkness. The lamplights of Manhattan Beach guided my way as I lengthened my stride and short breaths in the winter air, frantically racing alongside the ocean. My trust in the center was crumbling.

Is the treatment team offering false promises? Are their methods safe? Can I really escape my tortured life? Is there strength inside this body or should I submit to my ED voice forever? Maybe it's better to live with anorexia than to face unbearable fullness and my horrific feels.

For an hour I manically raced along the path, venting my frustrations to the stars, still sparkling in the same peaceful way they had on cold Oregon nights decades before, as Shawn pointed out constellations from the safety of a roaring campfire. Eventually, as I continued to deeply inhale salty air and felt the calming forces of the sky and ocean, the pain in my belly and rage in my brain simultaneously subsided. I slackened my pace and felt serenity cascading over my troubled body. The chili was over; I had survived a significant challenge and a yellow brick road of hope and health lay ahead. Mal might momentarily overtake my thoughts, but every day I was discovering additional light and truth. Maybe I didn't need to become a *perfect* star in the sky! If I could overcome my doubts, fears, and limiting beliefs, I could diffuse love into the universe simply by shining my joyful spirit outwards. I was currently eating three meals and three snacks a day, something I never thought possible. Surely I was as strong as my surfer chick team leader with the dolphin tattoo. If she could live as an emancipated woman, free of anorexia and flooding her world with loving vibes, couldn't I fully recover too? Blowing warmth into my hands, I smiled towards the heavens and followed the streetlights home as dark waves rhythmically crashed into the beach.

~

I was on my way to releasing my true self. Cody insisted I was happier than ever before, and there were moments I looked at my naked body with acceptance, even with the addition of extra pounds. Rather than running away or distracting myself with movies or adventures, I was owning my recovery and furiously churning cream into butter. After projectile-vomiting kidney beans, I began achieving glorious (and far less messy) victories on the food front. I honored morning hunger cues, felt triumphant rather than defeated after lunch, and mastered the art of post-dinner self-soothing.

Still, the chili had taken its toll. Seeds of doubt lay under my optimistic surface, and although I ignored these small misgivings over the ensuing weeks, bit by bit my skeptical thoughts rooted deep into rich soil. First, there was a trip to see a gastrologist about stomach pains that mirrored my Xi'an intestinal symptoms and, ironically, flared-up after a Spicy Sesame Citrus Chicken Bao lunch. Fortunately, rather than a spontaneous endoscopy to investigate my intestinal tract, I simply received a doctor's note permitting me to skip out on future spice challenges. Swinging past the front desk on my way out, a nurse handed over a visit summary. "KA-BOOM!" went my heart as I spotted my weight, printed in bold at the top of the page. How could the nurse be so careless? She knew I was recovering from anorexia and absolutely could not know my weight, and yet there it was in black and white to destroy my week. Hot tears rising, my fury diverted from the doctor's office to my treatment team.

How can this weight increase on my small frame be healthy? Why am I expected to eat food my sensitive gut cannot process? What other challenges am I facing that are detrimental to my health?

A week later, a chocolate-covered almond incident cracked my trust completely. It was a gorgeous spring morning and I was walking on clouds after having devoured a strawberry pastry, vanilla yogurt, a banana, and a glass of chocolate almond milk. Usually, in the safety of my home, I skimped on breakfast assignments, pitching out a piece of toast here or half a bruised banana there. But not today! This morning, for the first time in years, I woke up ravenous and ready to demolish a four-course meal. It was finally happening; I was recovering and, consequently, staring at a pastel array of foods evoked calm emotions. No, more than that—a spread of pink and creamy colors across my table looked marvelous! Rejoicing over this unexpected win as I strided through the center's avocado door, I smiled while mindlessly completing my daily meal form. A few hours later, however, a mandatory mid-morning snack killed my buzz. I wasn't a bit hungry! Instantly lamenting my recent feast, I questioned the magnitude of my breakfast requirements if I was expected to eat a snack so soon thereafter. Why did I need this snack? Why must I learn to eat when I am full? Isn't that why so many Americans are obese today? Would I eventually become obese too? I might have sucked up my angst if I'd selected an apple with peanut butter that morning. But, without carefully reviewing my options, I'd ticked my usual go-to: a half-cup of chocolate-covered almonds.

OMG, what have I done! I can't eat these now! I'm not Buddy the Elf; I can't eat pastries and chocolate-milk followed by almonds covered in chocolate! Why did I choose these for a snack today? What can I do?

Shaking with fear but without an escape route, I swallowed my half-cup as quickly as possible and promptly collapsed onto the brown sectional to cry it out. My tribe had never witnessed my tears before, and immediately rushed into my arms with reassuring words. Deriving comfort from their strength, I released my anguish as we embraced in a love huddle. These girls understood how chocolate-covered almonds could crack your heart on a Wednesday morning, and I was grateful for our ED kinship. But, losing my grip on Recovery, I requested a meeting with Alice that afternoon to challenge her methods, demanding details about my weight plan and an explanation as to why Recovery required an intolerably high daily intake.

"I'm already in a safe weight band according to the BMI," I charged. "I don't need to eat so much food. Your way doesn't seem safe or healthy; I feel like a bird, stuffed to excess for the sheer sake of stuffing."

"You haven't relinquished your control yet, Rachel," she retorted. "You must break through your food rules and the rigid boundaries you have abided for years. You must learn to accept feelings of fullness and trust that you are safe, regardless of the volume in your stomach. Eventually your weight will become a number, rather than how you define yourself, and you will be ready to live a recovered life. You must trust the process."

But I couldn't trust the process. Completely relinquishing all control to my treatment team—especially in the food sphere —was too much to ask. In all honesty, I wasn't sure if I was willing to accept a higher number on my scale in exchange for mental freedom. I wanted to be cured, but I still craved thinness; I longed to eat my Recovery cake and not eat it too. With competing perspectives dogging my steps in the subsequent weeks, I absorbed mental gems in sessions, but skimped on my pastel breakfasts, squeezed in forbidden hikes on the drive home, and requested to be released back into the wild ASAP.

∾

The six weeks I spent at an ED center were the hardest weeks of my life. The pain of ingesting thousands of calories a day after years of counting out almonds, and the pain of restless legs at midnight when you're accustomed to burning out your quads and hammies each day, cannot be measured. That said, I wish I had stuck it out! I wish I had kept popping chocolate-covered almonds and forced myself to break through the confines of my skinny jeans to face a sky-high number on the scale. If I had surrendered my mind *and* body to my treatment team, calories and weight might have become meaningless numbers in my life sooner rather than later. I might have accepted that mental health is far superior to a skinny frame and tucked into my Recovery cake with the knowledge our bodies have our backs, and that we can be active and fit without sacrificing our well-being. The thing is, there was a miscommunication; I never truly understood Alice's rationale behind my caloric requirements. It's only today, years later, that I comprehend the center's long-term, holistic philosophy:

*Fully relinquish your control **now** so that you can **eventually** enjoy an emancipated life! Eat an array of pastel colored treats and chocolate-covered almonds **now** so that you can **eventually** maintain a sustainable, nutritious lifestyle!*

I was impatient to have it all. I expected to become a fully recovered woman within two months and at a minimal cost.

This was stunningly unrealistic. Just like a severe acne medication, ED center life gets far worse before it gets better. You have to face your worst fears and feel your worst feels; you have to find comfort in a sea of discomfort and accept that terrifying number on a scale or acid-reflux might just be a crappy part of the process. Fortunately, once I lost my nerve and bolted home, a pathway to Recovery still shone in the distance.

26

WITNESSING TRUTH
LOS ANGELES, CALIFORNIA: AGE 33

Two weeks free of chocolate-covered almonds, I strolled along Manhattan Beach, watching mini sandpipers dash to and fro as I reassessed the value of treatment. Was I a changed woman advancing towards health and happiness or was Recovery a pie in the sky ideal for teenage anorexics and dreamers? I was certainly different from the woman staring down a PB&J beside Cody two months before. There was a bit more fullness in my cheeks and my belly was softer, but most significantly I'd burrowed into layers of decrepit insecurities and false constructs in group therapy with the support of my tribe to reclaim a vital, core truth:

I am good enough.

Accepting this truth meant everything! It meant I could stop proving myself worthy of love by chasing perfection—an elusive ideal that would never bring me happiness. It also meant I could rest safely in my skin, knowing my soul is valuable, with or without gold stars or approval. Sure, after years of restricting and hyper-producing to demonstrate excellence I wasn't instantly oozing chill vibes, and I still craved the feelings of thinness and physical exhaustion. My brain was hardwired to maintain a stringent existence, and, like an influx of bikini sales adverts after your Cancun vaca is cancelled, Mal couldn't help but dispatch the same tiresome ideas and commands as always. Now, however, I recognized her cries as outdated drivel I must practice ignoring until her voice became like the roar of a lion cub whose fierceness is met with an amused and sympathetic smile.

As part and parcel of Mal's fall from grace and a rediscovery of my worth was a Comeback Kid story of my true self. Finally—after rare busts into various scenes over the years—I recognized my childhood spirit as my true essence and disempowered Mal to place this joyful being at the forefront of my mind. Infused with courage and understanding, I was emancipated—free of anorexia's chains and ready to chase health and happiness as a dedicated love junkie. Yes, I mused, as my toes met cold, lapping waves, and sandpipers scurried about on hard-packed sand, I was immensely different from the frazzled woman staring down a PB&J just weeks before.

A lot of tough work still lays ahead, and I'm still frightened of weight and fullness, but Recovery is not an illusion and I am already well on my way.

~

I instinctively loved Anne, a woman with substantial ED expertise and a cheerful yet calm aura. I'd arranged this dietician appointment weeks before at the behest of my treatment team, all of whom were concerned about my hasty departure and eager to ensure I continued in a forward trajectory beyond the center's walls. As I settled into her buttery soft leather couch and launched into my ambition to become an "intuitive eater",

Anne crossed one stylish boot over the other and tucked a mischievous blonde strand behind her ear.

"I feel like I've maintained a safe weight since leaving the center," I asserted. "Rather than religiously sticking to Alice's post center diet plan, I'd like to nourish my body based on my cravings and hunger cues."

"Well Rachel," she thoughtfully responded, "If you are planning to eat intuitively so soon, you'll need to evaluate your trust levels. Do you trust yourself to respond to your body's needs? After battling your stomach for years, are you prepared to rebuild this relationship by treating yourself with loving kindness?"

Anne shuffled through a black filing cabinet while I pondered her question, locating a folder with print-outs of dietician Linda Omichinski's hunger and fullness scale. She recrossed one boot over the other and handed me a copy.

"Here; so long as you are still receiving hunger cues, this chart will help you identify and respond to your body's signals."

Quickly looking over the chart's sliding scale, I instantly recognized Number 1 as my home base through adulthood:

1: Beyond hungry. You may have a headache. You can't concentrate and feel dizzy. You may have trouble with coordination. You are totally out of energy and need to lie down. This may happen during a very restrictive diet.

"You should never reach the Number 1 or Number 2 point," Anne kindly advised. "Do you feel prepared to eat a snack if you reach Number 4 during the day?"

4: You start to think about food. Your body is giving you the signal that you might want to eat. You are a little hungry.

I paused for a moment, leaning forward towards Anne as I honestly and vulnerably confided in this seemingly warm-hearted woman.

"I believe so; I think so right now at least. But it will be hard to feel I deserve to eat before I reach a Number 3 on the scale."

"Hmm. Can you picture yourself as a little girl?" she asked, coughing lightly as she reached for a nearby glass of water.

Absolutely. In an instant I pictured myself in Oregon, racing back and forth through a sprinkler in a pink swimsuit while, across the yard, white sheets billowed as my mom clipped clothespins on their ends in a light breeze. I felt protected, happy, relaxed, and comfortable.

"Doesn't that little girl deserve a snack?" Anne continued, encouraged by my smile and silent nod. "Doesn't she *deserve* to be well-fed and satisfied? Can you imagine denying her?"

My childhood was jam-packed with blissful food memories. The blue tin filled with small stacks of buttery sugar cookies. A creamy blackberry milkshake after a hot day of U-Picking. Spoonfuls of strawberry jam filling the craters of golden Elephant Ears. Plump jammy donuts gleaming with sugary goodness in a bustling German bakery. My little self felt loved and valued. She knew ice cream should be licked on a summer's day simply because it tastes delicious. I blinked and saw my piggie-tailed self once more. This time she was standing in an abandoned yard with sharp blades of yellow grass scratching up against exposed toes. Alone and destitute, she looked at me with hungry eyes.

"Of course not; I wouldn't deny her anything," I solemnly responded.

"No? Well then, why do you deserve to be denied nutrients as an adult? Why don't you deserve to be well-nourished every day of your life?"

Painful moments of restriction and denial, some still raw enough to elicit bitter tears, flashed through my mind, to include: wrestling with hunger at university, sobbing into empty pizza boxes in New York and London, and racing towards the Skytrain in Vancouver as my gut cried out for breakfast. As Anne swiftly came to the rescue with a tissue, I lamented how much I had sacrificed in the name of skinny perfection. I had withheld so much compassion for this small girl in adult form, raking myself across hot coals of starvation and hyper-producing to achieve unrealistic, unhealthy, and completely unnecessary goals. It was a tragedy, but, fortunately, it wasn't the end of my story. After nearly two decades of mental and physical angst, I'd bravely taken steps towards Recovery and was currently reawakening to liberating truths. Anne's perfectly timed self-love gem resonated and lingered on my person as I pushed myself out of her supple leather couch, reached for my jean jacket, and nestled my purse strap onto my shoulder. Like a treasure seeker, this gem was exactly what I didn't know I needed on my journey. This was the second half of my core truth I could hold onto forever:

*I am good enough and **I deserve to be happy**.*

Standing up and softly smiling, I hugged Anne, wished her a lovely week, and headed back into the sunshine to face the day.

EPILOGUE
DEL MAR, CALIFORNIA: AGE 37 (4 YEARS LATER)

An awful lot has happened since I left Anne's office to continue on my journey towards Recovery. I've added job descriptions to my colorful resume, road-tripped across America with Brandon to reinforce our friendship, wished Cody a lifetime of happiness and laughter on his respective journey, and slipped farther down the coast to live in beautiful Del Mar. I've also kissed my gram farewell until we meet in heaven, reunited with Cambridge friends to celebrate a girlfriend's marriage, and fallen in love with the hottest of hot yoga classes. Best of all, I've danced under a sky full of stars and dined on red velvet cake to celebrate my vows to Ryan, the unexpected love of my life I absolutely adore. Now, as summer makes way for autumn breezes, I'm awed and humbled by the knowledge I will soon become a mother. I would have never dreamed when I googled "Anorexia Centers Los Angeles" years ago I'd be happily married, fifteen pounds pregnant and growing, and waking up most mornings with a peaceful heart. After years of binging, restricting, and thrashing my spirit with hateful words, I believed my health was far too damaged to entertain such happy notions.

Miraculously, however, our bodies are resilient soul shelters, designed to heal our wounds and to provide us with fresh blood and renewed strength to courageously forge ahead down bright and sometimes daunting paths. Likewise, our souls are poised and ready to recover from the deepest of wounds to send our true selves free into a sky of possibilities. Consequently, if we choose love over hate, passionately pursuing health and happiness as dedicated love junkies, anything is achievable— even complete Recovery! In her insightful book *8 Keys to Recovery from an Eating Disorder*, ED advocate Carolyn Costin defines Recovery this way:

Being Recovered is when a person can accept his or her natural body size and shape and no longer has a self-destructive relationship with food or exercise. When you are recovered, food and weight take a proper perspective in your life, and what you weigh is not more important than who you are; in fact, actual numbers are of little or no importance at all. When recovered, you will not compromise your health or betray your soul to look a certain way, wear a certain size, or reach a certain number on a scale. When you are recovered, you do not use eating disorder behaviors to deal with, distract from, or cope with other problems.

Although I feel close to Carolyn's description, I am not there yet! Unsurprisingly, although I am less impacted by the numbers on my scale than ever before, the food piece trips me up from time to time as I battle temptations to ruminate after a meal or a creamy and dreamy cupcake. With every small blip and setback, however, I become stronger and more committed to moving forward. This is partly because I've come to realize that, like all those posters plastered in libraries of adventurers scaling mountains, Recovery is not a simple question of success or failure! Rather, it is all about the mini wins, enlightening epiphanies, unexpected truths, and empowering knowledge you collect along your way.

Hopefully, you've popped a few of my anecdotes and self-love gems into your satchel as useful insights to keep in mind. Personally, the most brilliant gem I possess is a core truth that I am good enough and deserve to be happy. This truth took root in my mind as I wrestled with self-love as a newly minted love junkie. I was so accustomed to berating myself every day that at times it felt silly, false, or ridiculous to treat myself kindly. As my truth soaked into my soul completely, however, and I regained trust in myself, I began to manifest self-love by positively responding to ED thoughts, recognizing my worth as a perfectly imperfect woman (rather than comparing myself to Sylvian goddesses), accepting and dishing out compliments, and regularly affirming that I deserve respect, kindness, breaks, snacks, friends, naps, and plenty of satisfying meals. And slowly, gradually, after months and years of constant effort, the clouds lifted. My mind became clearer, my heart became calmer, my laughter became richer, my body became stronger, and I began to feel something I'd rarely experienced since childhood: pure JOY.

Joy is an incredible emotion that is available to all of us! It isn't found in skinny jeans, trips to Mexico, fancy dinner reservations, a thrilling Netflix series, or even a sparkly pair of earrings; rather, Joy is a deep happiness that comes from within. Although it can slip into our hearts and minds in stunning, present moments, I believe this intense emotion is best realized after we free ourselves from whatever darkness holds us captive. As emancipated love junkies, our hearts are open to experiencing Joy as we create love-centered existences that nurture and promote our well-being.

Consequently, regardless of your current rapport with your body, your food, your mind, and others, take heart! There is always hope, there is always a next step towards love, and there is always someone waiting for you to reach out to support you on your journey towards complete Recovery. You can start today—right this minute—to manifest self-love by offering yourself compassion for the beautiful soul you are. You can repair relationships with friends, family, and most importantly, yourself. We are all stronger than we believe and capable of churning the deepest of cream into the most delicious and hard-packed sweet butter. And, as we churn and churn as brave love junkies, we can dance, sing, laugh, and inspire others to release their true selves into the universe.

ABOUT RACHEL

Rachel is an Emancipated Love Junkie and hopes this book has helped you become one too! Currently living in Del Mar, California, she is happiest writing in coffee shops, going out to the movies, and biting into fresh donuts after coastal runs with her husband. If you enjoyed Rachel's first book, please support her work by writing a review here (thank you so much!): http://www.Amazon.com/gp/customer-reviews/write-a-review.html?asin=Bo8C8R6QPG http://rachelwilshusen.com/

Made in the USA
Columbia, SC
12 October 2020

22632012R00119